CONTENT TIPS FOR SERVICE BASED EXPERTS:

90 Days of Content Ideas to Captivate & Convert Your Ideal Clients With Ease

JAIMIE SARAH

authors
AND CO.

DISCLAIMER:

The author claims no legal basis, affiliation or paid relationship with the following platforms:

Facebook, Meta, Instagram, Linkedin

References in the publication are for information purposes only.

ISBN13 Paperback: 979-8-364200-21-1

ISBN13 Hardback: 978-1-915771-07-0

CONTENTS

Part Three
CLIENT CASE STUDIES AND TESTIMONIALS

Part Four
FACTS AND FIGURES

Part Six
OFFERS

DEDICATION

Thank you to my friends, family, mentors and clients. You inspire me every day.

And thank you to you, the reader, for picking up this book!

FOREWORD

This book is for brilliant experts like you who want to post more and better content online without getting stuck in a scroll hole or spending hours agonising over what to say.

It's a trusty friend you can call upon in those moments when you're simply not sure what to post even though you know you *should* be, or want to be, posting! It's a quick exit from uncertainty, guilt and confusion and a quick entry to clarity, confidence and consistency. It's also a tool you can call upon when batch-creating content, if you wish.

This book is suitable for you whether you are a small or medium-sized business owner, a marketer in a corporate marketing department or a professional who simply wants to start cultivating your personal brand online.

Attention spans in the world are shorter than ever right now, so it's not only important for *you* to be able to hold *your* attention with *creating* content, it's also critical to be able to create the kind of content that is truly going to capture your audience's attention — and in turn to convert them into paying customers or clients.

Otherwise, you might as well be spraying your favourite perfume while standing in the middle of a tornado. It might smell nice for a few seconds but it's not going to achieve the desired effect.

Let's be clear here, this is not just about creating vanity content that gets lots of "likes". It's about creating content that enables your ideal clients to get to know, like and trust you, leading them to actually hand over and trust you with their money and with their custom. Because *this* is the true art.

I've worked with thousands of service-based businesses over the past 15 years, mostly in the legal, financial, information technology, coaching and consulting industries, to help them attract and convert more clients — and not just any clients but their ideal clients. Their true target market.

Regardless of which industry you are in or which segment of the market you are looking to captivate and convert, great content is an integral piece of the puzzle to achieving these goals.

This book will help you use your content creation time most efficiently and avoid getting sucked into social media reactivity when there are other business and marketing priorities to focus on.

You can also apply the ideas in this book to non-social marketing channels, for example emails, blog-posts, PR, talks etc., however, I refer to social media throughout this book simply for ease of application.

I hope you enjoy it and I can't wait to hear how you get on! If you want to share a win you've had from using the book, please feel free to email me at hello@jaimiesarah.com or tag me on your favourite social media platform!

Instagram: www.instagram.com/definitely_definitely

Facebook: www.facebook.com/definitelydefinitely

LinkedIn: www.linkedin.com/in/jaimiesarah

If you're posting using the tips, feel free to include the hashtag #90daysofcontent so I can see the great things you're creating!

Jaimie

P.S. If you'd like to work with me further, check out my website www.jaimiesarah.com where you can learn about other ways I can support you in attracting and retaining more ideal clients. This includes my low-cost membership, close-knit mastermind, 1-1 consulting and "done for you" agency services.

HOW TO USE THIS BOOK

The suggestions in this book pertain to six key categories of content that I've created and tested over many years and that I find work well for the majority of my clients, all of whom are service-based experts.

I recommend alternating between the categories in equal measure. For example - posting a piece of connection content one day, a piece of story-based content the following day, a client testimonial the following day, a fact or figure the following day, an authority-building piece of content the day after that, and an offer the day after that. This is just a guideline, and obviously, if you're posting multiple pieces a day you can move through this rotation or cycle more quickly.

Just be sure not to post too many consecutive pieces of content in the same category, or to post only from one or two of the categories. This is a common mistake that can kill engagement and conversions, no matter how brilliant you or your company is at meeting your clients' needs!

For example, if you post too much consecutive connection content, it is likely that your audience will really want to be friends with you (cue endless requests to "meet for coffee" or be "biz besties"!), but they might not have a clue what you actually do or what they could buy from you.

If you post too much story-based content, you may appear as a highly-qualified pontificator (or indeed a great storyteller) but again, your audience may not necessarily be clear exactly how or why you can help them solve the problem or problems your services can help them solve.

Too many client testimonials or too many offer posts back to back can appear as overly "pitchy", "trying too hard", or "needy".

Too much authority building content can lead your audience to think you are very smart and qualified, but they may not feel a connection to you or your brand on a personal/human level, which is becoming increasingly important these days, even for the biggest of corporate brands.

(Virgin is an example of one of the biggest brands in the world striking the authoritative yet fun and human balance incredibly well, in my opinion.)

If you have a small business based on a personal brand, you might have some degree of fear or resistance around posting content that isn't connection or story-based. You may have got very comfortable with connection and story-based content but more "corporate" or "salesy" forms of content may feel more alien to you, or you may have some fear underneath the surface that your audience will run away if you become more authoritative and/or make more offers publicly. My recommendation: observe this with curiosity, and do it anyway.

Done right, this will not happen. Not if your audience is truly "your" target audience. Not with your ideal clients.

Nevertheless, sometimes when implementing a more authoritative range of content or increasing the quantity of your content, just as with ramping up almost any form of marketing, it's not only possible but likely that there will be a small percentage of people that get triggered.

Triggered that you are saying more, triggered that you are saying too much, triggered that you are marketing, triggered that you are existing, triggered that you are breathing... I think you get the picture.

This is an important thing to make peace with, whether the brand you are representing is personal or corporate. If you haven't been posting content a lot or have been posting infrequently, or have been posting only "fluffy" content... or simply just because you appear in someone's feed or email inbox in the wrong moment when they are stressed about something that has absolutely nothing to do with you.... *some* people will not respond well. (These people are usually not your ideal clients, however.)

Unsubscribes, unfollows, negative responses etc., are good things to have an awareness of as sometimes they can provide useful "market feedback" when you are veering off-brand or have "misread the room", but don't obsess over them. The bigger your audience, the more the statistical likelihood of at least SOME adverse reactions, no matter how captivating and compelling your content is.

Remember to stay focused on the bigger goals, stay strategic — and keep going no matter what! Quantity and quality are *both* important in the game of captivating and converting ideal clients.

If you are particularly time-pressured or under a lot of stress, this is all the more reason to batch-create and pre-schedule your content and this book will help you do exactly that.

I'm going to cover six categories of content in this book. Let me tell you a bit more about each of them before we jump in.

The 6 Types of Content To Captivate and Convert™

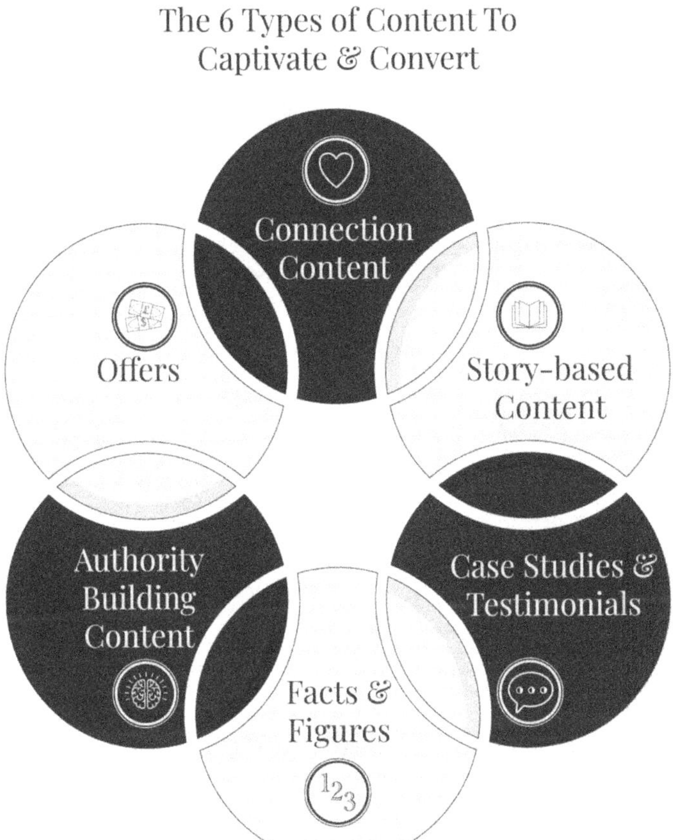

1. CONNECTION CONTENT

Connection content is things like sharing your (or your brand's) heart, feelings, values, hopes and dreams.

---

2. STORY-BASED CONTENT

Story-based content is things like sharing your personal or company story, your professional experiences, growth journey and milestones. This can also be used to share reflections, breakthroughs and "behind the scenes" scenarios in a way that humanises your brand.

---

3. CLIENT CASE STUDIES AND TESTIMONIALS AKA "BUZZ"

These are things like screenshots from customer messages or emails, comments on social media, as well as formal testimonials on review sites, and even excerpts from longer-form case studies. If it's from a customer, it's positive, and you have their consent to share, it goes here!

---

4. FACTS AND FIGURES

These are things like "did you know" statistics and numbers relevant to your zone of genius. For example, industry statistics, risks or costs associated with not using your services, or from getting it wrong, and indeed the quantitative benefits from getting it right with the help of your services.

---

5. AUTHORITY BUILDING CONTENT

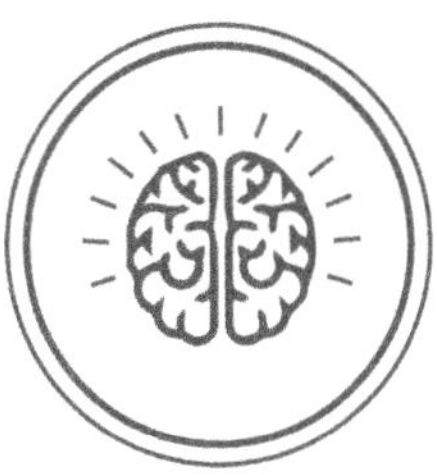

Authority-building content is things like standalone tips, advice and lessons relevant to your zone of genius and services. These will often be things that a person or company might be scared to share for fear of "giving it all away" but actually unless you're giving your actual services away, there isn't really such a thing. All other things being equal, the more authority building content there is out in the world from your brand, the better.

---

6. OFFERS

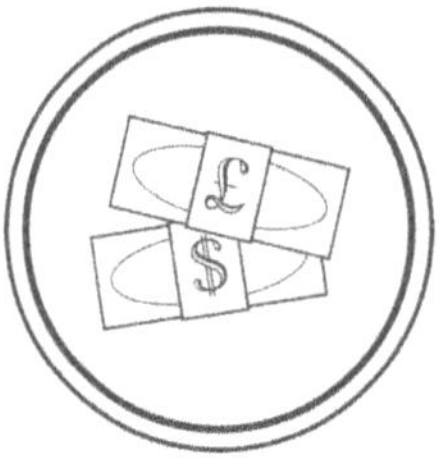

This is the piece many forget! The other categories of content are all very well, but if you aren't making offers regarding your services, how will your ideal clients know what and how to buy from you? Don't forget this piece! This includes: reminding your followers about your services, including links to buy new or existing services, making time-limited promotional offers, offering free trials and more.

Can you already see where your brand might have been over-relying on one or two of these categories and not having enough of a breadth of content? If so, you're in the perfect place as I'm going to give you a bunch of ideas to correct your course.

And if you're already covering these 6 types of content, you're still in the perfect place as you'll get some new ideas to continue onwards.

Lastly, I want to note that it's possible to create individual pieces of content that speak to two, or three or more of these types of content all in one piece - this is a wonderful thing too.

So are you ready? Let's do this!

You can start at the beginning of the book, or just open any page at random, whatever works for you!

Part One

CONNECTION CONTENT

Connection content is things like sharing your (or your brand's) heart, feelings, values, hopes and dreams.

1

GIVE YOUR AUDIENCE A LITTLE BEHIND-THE-SCENES OF YOUR DAY

SHARE a selfie or video of what you're up to and where and what's on your schedule for the day. Then invite them to share how they're spending their day too and/or wish them a fabulous day. If you are in a corporate marketing department, this can be a spotlight on a different senior leader or department, for example the CEO, the "product development team" or the "customer service team". You can make this a regular item (for example, every Friday, or the first Monday of each month), and highlight a different person or team each week.

Why this matters:

It shows your audience and ideal clients that you're a real person/people, with real faces and a real schedule, and makes them feel closer to you. People like to buy from people they feel like they know, like and trust. They can't do those things if they're not seeing you.

2

SHARE A PICTURE OF YOUR PET, OR OFFICE DOG!

Say something cute, like "good morning from Bob and I/us!". Bonus points if you and your pet are both wearing a cheesy grin!

Why this matters:

Everyone loves pets… except serial killers, so not only is this an easy way to filter out potential clients who you don't want to be servicing, but looking at cute animals is good for people's brains. It boosts the release of dopamine and oxytocin which makes people feel more warm and fuzzy, which in turn they will attribute to you and your brand.

(The same can be true by the way for babies and young children, although this can be a more love/hate topic depending on individual client/audience members' lifestyles and past experiences.)

3

SHARE A PICTURE OF YOUR DESK OR OFFICE* AND SHARE SOMETHING YOU'RE LOOKING FORWARD TO TODAY

For example, a selfie of you at your desk with the caption "Looking forward to helping some brilliant clients {achieve X} today!" You might then want to go into more detail, for example sharing what your rough agenda or journey for the day looks like en route to this objective!

*Important: ONLY share a picture of your desk or office if it's tidy - messy desks or chaotic backgrounds are a big no-no for any professional (especially high-level or prestigious) brand, unless you're in construction/property or are an artist sharing "before and after" pictures. Only share chaotic pictures in the context of "before and after".

Why this matters:

A post like this connects your audience with your work ethic and expertise as well as the outcomes you can help them with. Almost nobody will see every single piece of content you or your brand posts, so this keeps your expertise front of mind for new and old followers alike, and increases the likelihood that when they or someone they know is facing a problem or goal that your services can help with, you will be the first to come to mind! Sharing the journey can also bring the process to life and provide reassurance that there is an organised structure underpinning what you do.

4

SHARE A PICTURE OF YOUR OFFICE VIEW WITH A FUNNY COMMENT

FOR EXAMPLE "What is the meaning of life? I'm not sure but this pigeon outside my/our office window looks like he knows! Wishing you all a great Monday from {company name} HQ!". Make it something slightly silly and/or tongue-in-cheek philosophical that genuinely makes you and others laugh and smile.

Why this matters:

Humour is highly magnetic (especially on a Monday morning, ha!). Try to keep it light-hearted and accessible humour, don't veer into controversial/polarising humour unless that's truly aligned with your brand values. The quantity of humorous content that will be aligned for your brand will depend on your specific niche, ideal client and brand values, but at least a *little* bit of humour is good for almost all brands.

5

SHARE A TEAM/INDIVIDUAL SELFIE EN ROUTE TO A CLIENT VISIT OR EVENT AND CONNECT IT BACK TO YOUR CUSTOMER OUTCOMES

THIS MIGHT SAY for example "Excited to help one of our clients {get more X} today!". As per tip 3, you can then go into more detail regarding the process if you wish, or keep it mysterious! You might also want to share a recent very specific and tangible result you've helped said client (or a similar client or clients) attain.

Hint: Make sure you ask for your client's permission first if you're sharing anything that could be construed as confidential information, for example, client/company names, nature of how you're helping them and so on. If you have a legal department, further check that there is not an NDA in place with the company. Maintain a list of clients with NDAs and clients without, and always have express permission from individual contacts to share too. Some companies can be highly sensitive to being mentioned even anonymously. This helps keep the relationship safe and secure.

Why this matters:

Sharing the kind of work you do with clients, even if keeping it vague for confidentiality reasons, brings to life that you are a real-life human or humans, creating an impact in the world. It also conveys enthusiasm and passion for your work and for being of service, which is highly magnetic. Again it also connects your audience with the outcomes you help provide which helps you be front of mind if they or someone they know needs or wants these outcomes. It also speaks to natural human curiosity about what it is that you do day to day.

6

SHARE BEHIND THE SCENES OF A CLIENT VISIT, EVENT OR RETREAT

THIS MIGHT BE a picture or a video. Share a visual and then let your audience know what the agenda looks like i.e., what's taken place and what's happening next. (Without giving it *all* away - leave at least *some* space for mystery.)

Hint: If you're running an event or retreat, it's a good idea to have all attendees sign a release form on arrival which gives you permission to use footage from the event as you wish. This is important because whilst sharing content is important for acquiring new clients, so is making your existing clients feel safe and respected when it comes to any content containing or mentioning them.

Why this matters:

With this content, you are feeding the spirit of natural human curiosity. Human beings love to get sneaky peeks about what's going on behind the scenes! You're also painting a picture, so your ideal clients will naturally imagine what it would be like to be working with you in this capacity or in this particular setting. They will wonder what it will be like to have experienced X or be about to experience Y, this can often trigger FOMO and enquiries for future client visits, events or retreats. Be sure to also include a link to join the waitlist or register for a future event here or shortly thereafter!

7

SHARE A TEAM/INDIVIDUAL SELFIE AFTER A CLIENT VISIT

THIS MIGHT SAY something like "Our {X} team had a brilliant day today visiting our client {Y}. We are so excited to be partnering with them to improve their {Z}." Or "Today we worked with a client on {A, B and C} and they were delighted with the outcome!"

Why this matters:

Sharing the kind of work you/your company does and the outcomes it results in for your clients on a regular basis really brings your work and impact to life for those who are considering hiring you or buying your company's services. It also conveys enthusiasm and a service-oriented mindset, which is highly magnetic.

Share as much as you can without breaching privacy or making a client feel compromised. Another option is to anonymise the client. For example "Our team had a brilliant day with one of our FTSE 100 clients today, who we are so excited to be partnering with to improve the efficiency of their {X} function. To find out more about how we could help you, visit www.howwecanhelpyoutoo.com"

8

SHARE A TEAM PHOTO AT YOUR CHRISTMAS OR SUMMER PARTY OR SOCIAL EVENT

SHARE A SMART, happy team photo (no tequila shots haha, sorry!) and acknowledge everyone for their efforts. Reiterate how great it is to be surrounded by people who really care about your customers and mission — and about each other too!

Why this matters:

A post like this speaks to a spirit of unity, harmony and gratitude inside your company culture, and this is very magnetic. People are naturally more drawn to happy, grateful and frictionless people and businesses. Your clients and potential clients also like to know that you genuinely care about your mission and each other. By extension, this gives them the sense that being your client is going to be a happy experience too!

9

REMIND YOUR AUDIENCE OF YOUR MISSION

For example "At {company name} we stand for / we believe in {mission statement/brief description of your mission}. Are you with us?". Better still if this includes a picture or selfie next to a poster or decal of your mission statement on your office wall!

Why this matters:

Even if you've posted a piece of content about your mission and / or company values before, it never hurts to *remind* your audience what you stand for. Plus, hopefully, there are new people joining your audience all the time who may not have heard you share about it before!

This helps your client and prospective clients feel connected to the heart of your business. That you aren't simply a profit-extracting machine but a company on a mission to make the world better in your own special way. When people know what you stand for, this tends to result in greater brand loyalty.

10

ACKNOWLEDGE A FEW PEOPLE WHO HAVE HELPED OR UPLIFTED YOUR COMPANY THIS WEEK

THIS MIGHT BE SUPPLIERS, friends, family, random strangers — whatever is in alignment with your brand. Acknowledge a few different people and tag them publicly to thank them for their efforts and support.

Why this matters:

Acknowledging others shows a spirit of reciprocity and kindness that warms your audience's heart. When their heart feels warm because of you, they are more likely to know, like and trust you. This, in turn, makes them more likely to buy from you/your company. And not just once, but over and over and over.

Oh, and it creates a ripple of positive energy too — one which can be directly tracked back to you! People will forget what you did, but they'll never forget how you made them feel. You might even inspire them to follow suit.

11

EXPRESS YOUR GRATITUDE FOR THE PEOPLE IN YOUR LIFE AND BUSINESS, WITHOUT WHOM YOU COULDN'T DO WHAT YOU DO

These can be team members, service providers, family, friends, or your partner. Express how grateful you are for their support and encouragement, ideally include photos with each person mentioned and tag them too.

Why this matters:

Gratitude is a really magnetic emotion. It's contagious too! When you share the things you are grateful for, your audience will also be inclined to think about what they might be grateful for too. An extension of simply acknowledging others, expressing gratitude really shows a warmth of spirit and appreciation that makes your audience gravitate towards you.

Once they've gravitated towards you, their curiosity about your services becomes heightened and the next natural step is, of course, to buy from you!

12

THANK YOUR FOLLOWERS/AUDIENCE FOR BEING HERE AND FOR CHOOSING TO STAY CONNECTED

This doesn't need to be an essay - a simple "thank you for sticking with us - your attention is valuable and we appreciate you!" can suffice.

Why this matters:

This tip is something many take for granted. Your audience doesn't have to keep following you, or engaging with your marketing. They make a choice to do so, or not to do so.

It's a nice gesture to acknowledge this and to recognise that their attention is something that you value. Everyone likes to feel appreciated for their choices. In business and life alike, we also tend to get more of what we appreciate.

13

SHARE SOMETHING THAT'S BEEN ON YOUR HEART THAT PERTAINS TO ONE OF YOUR DEEPEST VALUES

Have you been thinking about how lucky you are to get to spend time with your family without compromise? Have you been thinking about how much being in nature gets you out of your head and how much you're enjoying your new wild swimming habit? Perhaps you've been pondering your next trip or charitable activity? Share it!

Why this matters:

This kind of content demonstrates your leadership in being an expert and human who stands by their values and refuses to settle. This shows a steadfastness and integrity that can make you feel more trustworthy and reliable to your audience. Added bonus: you never know who you might inspire to make a change in their habits to better reflect their values and desires.

In a larger corporation, this could be a reflection from your CEO or a spotlight on a different leader on a regular basis (e.g. fortnightly/monthly) each sharing something that's on their heart that is relevant to your brand values.

14

SHARE A RANDOM ACT OF KINDNESS THAT YOU ENGAGED IN OR BENEFITED FROM THIS WEEK

IDEALLY INCLUDE a photo (or topic relevant photo) and a short story of what inspired or how it came about. Tag any relevant people. You might also want to remind your audience why random acts of kindness are good for people, and perhaps invite your followers to engage in one too!

Why this matters:

There's more to life than business and financial exchange. Sometimes it's nice to do something for someone simply because you felt called to. It's also really valuable to practice receiving. Giving and receiving freely are part of the flow and spirit of true abundance. When it comes to sharing acts of kindness you've initiated, this also showcases your generosity of spirit which again increases the "know, like and trust" factor, as it indicates that you are a "good" person and might well be generous with them too. This makes you more appealing as a service-provider than one who might be stingy or Scrooge-like, which is the opposite of magnetic!

15

MAKE A STAND FOR A CAUSE THAT YOU SUPPORT BASED ON YOUR/YOUR BRAND VALUES

It could be a run for charity, initiating a fundraiser or pledging a percentage of company profits to non-profits. Share something you or your company is doing to support a cause that you believe in and that aligns with your brand values. This could also mean donating your time or expertise to a charity, becoming an ambassador of a charity, or advocating for a change in legislation in local or national government.

Why this matters:

Activities and choices like this show that you are about more than just your own gain. They show that your company is about more than just capitalist objectives. They show that you are willing to stand for something. That you are invested in the greater good. That your brand values aren't just for show — they're things you live and breathe by. This speaks volumes about you and your brand, and can often be some of the best marketing you ever do — whether intended that way or not!

16

SHARE A HOPE OR DREAM THAT YOU HAVE FOR YOURSELF OR YOUR INDUSTRY

THIS MIGHT BE something you really want to change or the wider ripple effect you want your work to have. For example, a statement about the number of customers you want to impact: "reaching ten million households by 2030", or "helping 10,000 female entrepreneurs make £20k a month by 2025". Or it could be a wish that you have for people, such as "I dream of a world where all children have access to primary education" or "I stand for a world where all marketing is rooted in truth and ethics."

This works best when backed up with tangible actions, i.e., something that you are putting in place to support the fulfilment of this hope or dream. A product/service or offering that directly contributes to the outcome you mentioned, a profit pledge that contributes to the outcome — all show that your words are meaningful and devotional.

Why this matters:

This kind of content speaks to your/your company's ability to zoom out and see the bigger picture. It can also speak to an appreciation of the interconnectedness of humanity and our duty to look after each other, not simply to look after our own interests. If you want to attract customers and clients who care about the bigger picture, this is a great way to do so, as like attracts like. These statements can sometimes be incorporated into your brand message to amplify it too.

17

ASK AN INTERESTING QUESTION THAT SHOWS THAT YOU VALUE YOUR AUDIENCE'S PERSPECTIVE

For example, "If you could have dinner with anyone on earth, who would you choose?" Or this could be asking for input on your next charitable cause, or asking a question about something you're puzzled or unsure about.

Why this matters:

This demonstrates curiosity and a growth mindset. These are very appealing traits. People naturally want to spend more time with those who are curious and growth-oriented. If your question is about something you need help with, you'll also trigger the "helper's high" in those who respond, and the person helping will then associate with you and your brand with that high. Winner winner, chicken dinner!

18

RESPOND PROMPTLY

MAKE sure you (or one of your team) reply to as many comments as possible, and as promptly as possible so that your audience feels they really do matter and that you're listening as well as "talking". Have a system in place to manage this at least Monday to Thursday.

Why this matters:

No one likes talking to an empty room or a brick wall. The more you respond, the more you reward engagement and participation. This makes people want to keep coming back for more. It also means you're more likely to convert your leads since a faster response rate tends to be associated with a higher close rate. Makes sense to get them while they're hot, right?

Your audience will also assume that if you're responsive to their social media comments, you're probably quite responsive as a service provider too.

Part Two

STORY-BASED CONTENT

Story-based content is things like sharing your personal or company story, your professional experiences, growth journey and milestones. This can also be used to share reflections, breakthroughs and "behind the scenes" scenarios in a way that humanises your brand.

19

SHARE A STORY ABOUT SOMETHING THAT INSPIRED YOU RECENTLY

THIS MIGHT BE a talk or event you attended, a book you read, or an interaction or conversation that you had. Bonus points if it mirrors something your ideal client is thinking or a challenge they're having! Remember to tag any individuals or businesses that you're mentioning too.

Why this matters:

You're giving your audience the opportunity to piggyback on your inspiration and insights. You're demonstrating that you or your brand are continually moving forward, not standing still. You're demonstrating a spirit of growth and receptivity. This helps you attract clients who are also growth-oriented, and who will assume that your services will continually grow and improve too.

20

SHARE A STORY ABOUT SOMETHING THAT HELPED YOU GROW IN THE PAST THAT WAS HARD

THIS IS ESPECIALLY beneficial if you're talking about something that is directly relevant to the services or offerings your company provides. For example, a story about finding it really hard to {INSERT STRUGGLE OR CHALLENGE HERE}, really struggling with it and then finding the inspiration to create your company to help others overcome {INSERT STRUGGLE OR CHALLENGE AGAIN HERE}.

It doesn't always *have* to be relevant to your offerings, but whatever you share, remember to ask the question "is this on brand?" and also to talk "from the scab, not the wound" if talking about something painful. Again, bonus points if it mirrors something your ideal client would come to you to get a resolution on or to move forward on!

Why this matters:

With this kind of content, you're reminding your audience that growth is possible. You're reminding them that even hard things can be really fruitful. You're reminding them that success doesn't happen by magic or overnight. You're reminding them that hard things can be huge gifts in disguise. You're also connecting them to what's possible. And done right, you're making them fall a little bit in love with you and your resilient heart!

21

SHARE A STORY ABOUT SOMETHING THAT CHANGED YOU IN THE PAST THAT WAS A WONDERFUL SURPRISE FROM NOWHERE

THIS MIGHT BE A CHANCE ENCOUNTER, a sign from above, a surprise act of generosity or perhaps even a surprise visit. Whatever it is, make it a heartwarming story that will make people feel all warm and fuzzy inside!

Why this matters:

Warm, fuzzy stories with happy endings stimulate the release of dopamine and oxytocin which your audience will then associate with your brand. This is how your brand begins to feel like a lovely, warm hug! Bonus points if the story is directly relevant to your brand mission, and/or something that might reasonably happen to your ideal client, that leaves them with a real sense of possibility and hopefulness pertinent to your zone of genius.

22

ASK YOURSELF THE QUESTION, "WHAT PAST EXPERIENCES DO MY AUDIENCE NEED TO HEAR FROM ME ABOUT TODAY?"

SHARE a story about an experience that is directly relevant to your mission. For example, a goal you set yourself earlier on in life or business that, if you had the benefit of your services, would or could have been accomplished much sooner. Perhaps it's a story you heard. It could even be an interview with your CEO or a member of your leadership team pertaining to the company's evolution.

Why this matters:

A bit like with #21, you're creating a sense of possibility and hopefulness. You're creating a bridge between a challenge and a solution. This links you and your brand with the thought and frequency of "solutions" as well as with "progress" and "evolution". And this is a wonderful thing! You want your brand to be and to feel ever evolving. Stagnancy is the last thing you or your ideal clients want!

Hint: Stories of evolution can really help with *retaining* high-calibre clients too.

23

SHARE A STORY ABOUT A CUSTOMER

Now, you'll want to make this customer an ideal customer for maximum effect. Share a story about where they were before they engaged your services, and where they are now. What were the outcomes? What did they enjoy about the journey? What difference did it make having your services vs. before they had them? Did anything happen more rapidly? Was the ultimate outcome better? What impact did this have? What other impacts or side effects did this lead to?

The better the picture you can paint, the more valuable this will be! Either use the customer's name (plus company and industry, if useful) with their permission, or anonymise the story such that they can't be identified. (Note: it's still good practice to get their consent, even if they're anonymised.)

Why this matters:

A picture is worth a thousand words. This kind of story paints a picture of what's possible from engaging your services, with a clear before and after. The human brain loves this! Your ideal clients will naturally imagine themselves also attaining the "after" shared in your story, and this will increase their anticipation and sense of urgency around procuring your services.

24

SHARE A STORY ABOUT A LIFE LESSON YOU LEARNED RECENTLY

DID YOU LEARN A NEW SKILL? Did something not go to plan, but you learned something valuable you'll now take with you forever? Did something awful happen, but it ultimately connected you with the sanctity and beauty of life? With this kind of piece, it's a particularly good idea to run it by a trusted colleague, but done right, this kind of content can be both cathartic and deeply inspiring to your audience.

Why this matters:

Your audience gets to piggyback on your lesson, without having to experience the toil, challenges or turmoil you did. This makes them feel that you or your company is one that wants to help them fast track their success. You've done the hard work so they don't have to. This helps to build trust and rapport that just keeps them coming back for more. Just don't make the lesson too recent or too painful! Apply the rule "share the scab, not the wound" if it was a tough lesson, or this can damage your credibility and/or have your audience worrying about you. You want to leave them inspired, not concerned or anxious.

25

SHARE A STORY ABOUT A PROFESSIONAL LESSON YOU LEARNED RECENTLY

TELL a story about a recent professional lesson you learned. Did you learn about a new aspect of business you didn't know about before? Did you learn that revenue is vanity and profit is sanity?! Did you learn something quite technical that will resonate with your ideal client? Share away. Again run this one by a colleague or peer to check it resonates.

Why this matters:

Like with sharing a personal life lesson, your audience gets to piggyback on your learning and growth. This exudes a spirit of generosity and authenticity that makes them feel more trust and loyalty towards you. And you know what trust and loyalty lead to - buying behaviour!

26

SHARE A STORY ABOUT A RECENT CUSTOMER INTERACTION

TELL a story about a recent customer interaction. Perhaps a customer came to you feeling jaded and defeated in relation to your zone of genius, and you restored their faith and their hope that it "wasn't too late". Perhaps your non-judgmental approach and kindness inspired them to forgive themselves for not taking action earlier.

Share (with permission) this interaction. For example, "A client came to me today and she was tying herself in knots about not having got her {INSERT THING YOU HELP WITH} organised earlier. She felt so guilty and ashamed that she hadn't already done it. I explained how common this is and that it's nothing to be ashamed of and the most important thing is getting it sorted now. She breathed a huge sigh of relief and we {THING YOU HELPED CLIENT PUT IN PLACE OR RESOLVE}. She said she now feels like she has peace of mind for the first time in a long time. I'm so grateful to get to do this work!"

Why this matters:

With these kind of examples, you are painting a picture of how you and your company help and the emotional drawback of not having your help as well as the emotional benefits of having it. People usually don't make decisions purely for the rational benefits. They make decisions in no small part for the way they're going to feel later. This kind of story taps into that and evokes the feeling ahead of time, so that they can get a taste of what's possible!

27

SHARE A QUESTION YOU GET ALL THE TIME – AND THE ANSWER

FOR EXAMPLE, "My clients often ask me "{INSERT QUESTION THEY OFTEN ASK YOU}". Here's what I tell them: {INSERT THING YOU TELL THEM}." Then follow up with a conclusion, for example "So if you're wondering about this too, I just want you to know {THING YOU WANT THEM TO KNOW}. And if you'd like my help with this, just {INSERT YOUR CALL TO ACTION E.G., SEND ME A DM/CLICK THE LINK BELOW, ETC.}"

Why this matters:

Sharing client questions and answers does two things. It gives them a sense of being a "fly on the wall" which appeals to natural human curiosity. It also shows that you UNDERSTAND your clients and that you care about providing clear answers to their questions. One of the most important things to a potential client is that you and your company understands them and their concerns. They also want to know that you understand *how* to help them and will do so efficiently.

This kind of content helps them connect with that in a really simple way. You can use this for questions about the problem you help solve, questions about your service, questions about the outcomes of using your services, there are lots of possibilities here!

28

SHARE A "YOU MIGHT BE WONDERING STORY"

For example, "You might be wondering — is this for me? Well, let me tell you about my client Sarah, who came to me and wondered the same thing. She was tying herself in knots about {INSERT PAIN POINTS OF YOUR IDEAL CLIENT}, and wondering what was the best step forward. She looked at a view different options in the market and when she came to {ME/COMPANY NAME} she was looking for {INSERT THING YOUR IDEAL CLIENT REALLY WANTS}. We had a chat and I told her that our {INSERT SERVICE NAME} was PERFECT for her. That was {INSERT TIME PERIOD AGO} and now she's {INSERT TANGIBLE OUTCOME(S) OF USING SERVICE}."

Why this matters:

This kind of story shows that you deeply understand the pain points and desires of your ideal clients, and what pain points and desires your service or services are a great fit for. This provides a deep sense of clarity and confidence that if these are pain points and desires that are front of mind for them, you/your company are well-positioned to help. You're also providing an idea of time-frame which is valuable for those who are wondering how long things might take and for setting expectations accordingly.

29

TELL AN "OBJECTION INOCULATION" STORY

WITH THIS ONE, you're going to tell a story about an objection that a previous or current customer had, and how you handled it. For example, "When my client Bob came to me, he was worried that {INSERT OBJECTION}. He'd been burned before by other providers and really didn't want to waste any more money on solutions that didn't give him what he needed. I showed Bob {INSERT EVIDENCE TO COUNTER OBJECTION e.g. stats, figures, previous testimonials, 5-star ratings etc} and explained our {IF YOU HAVE A GUARANTEE OR SATISFACTION PROMISE ETC, DETAIL THAT HERE, IF NOT EXPLAIN WHAT YOU DO TO MAKE SURE YOUR CLIENTS ARE HAPPY}.

He breathed a big sigh of relief and he's been a customer/one of our top clients for {INSERT DURATION HE'S BEEN A CUSTOMER FOR HERE} now. {THEN ADD ANY OTHER OUTCOMES OF HIM/HIS COMPANY USING THE SERVICES HERE}.

Why this matters:

This story achieves two things. Firstly, it helps address a specific objection head on — the ethical way. (You can create a story like this for every objection you face, in fact, I recommend it!). Secondly, it provides a sense of evidence, or proof. This makes your customer feel safer and like there's less risk, perhaps even "nothing to lose" from buying your service. This will be especially true if there is some kind of service guarantee, satisfaction guarantee or "money back policy".

All other things being equal, these tend to dramatically increase conversion rates as well as making your customer feel more at ease and confident about the service. (This tends to translate to how they engage with the service later.) Do be warned though, if the service success requires input from them, make this clear. Guarantees *can* make some customers complacent! Make sure you have the appropriate disclaimers and/or disclosures in place to counter this.

30

TELL YOUR BRAND ORIGIN STORY

How and why did you or your company start doing what you do? Where did it all begin? What was your or your brand's initial vision? What was the mission? Has it changed at all? If so, how? What are a few of the highlights learned along the way? How do you understand your customers better now?

Why this matters:

Everyone loves a dream! Sharing your (or the founders') original hopes and dreams, and the evolution of these hopes and dreams over time, creates a deep sense of intimacy. Your audience begin to feel like a trusted confidant. They feel special. It almost conjures up a family vibe — where they feel part of your family or inner circle. This creates more attraction and loyalty to the brand. It also creates a sense of legacy and longevity that is really attractive. We like to buy from companies that are in it for the long-haul, and the higher calibre the client, the more true this is.

31

TELL A STORY ABOUT AN EMPLOYEE

TELL a story about an employee (if you're a solopreneur - this will be you!!) and what they do on a daily basis, what their favourite parts of their role are, how their role has changed and what they've learned along the way. Be sure to infuse their passion for making sure customers are happy/get great results into this story.

Why this matters:

You're bringing the brand to life. You're bringing your people — some or many of whom may be "behind the scenes" or may be taken for granted by your customers — to life. This means that when they're interacting with the company everything feels more personal. It can also translate to more respect, compassion and appreciation from clients towards your team.

32

TELL A STORY ABOUT YOUR LONGEST-SERVING EMPLOYEE/TEAM MEMBER

TELL a story about your longest-serving employee, what they do on a daily basis, what their favourite parts of their role are, how their role has changed and what they've learned along the way. Again, be sure to infuse their passion for the brand and for making sure customers are happy into this story.

Why this matters:

People buy people. You're conveying that your business is people. Real people. Who really care. And that loyalty works both ways. Your audience will also assume if employees stay with you a long time, that you treat your people well and ethically, that you are fair and just. This makes you more appealing to those to whom these values are important. The last thing your customers want to be doing is worrying about if a company they buy from is abusing or mistreating their employees! Not least because this usually translates to the customer experience eventually.

Part Three

CLIENT CASE STUDIES AND TESTIMONIALS

These are things like screenshots from customer messages or emails, comments on social media, as well as formal testimonials on review sites, and even excerpts from longer-form case studies. If it's from a customer, it's positive, and you have their consent to share, it goes here!

33

SHARE THE BRILLIANT WORK YOU (OR ONE OF THE TEAM) JUST DID WITH A CLIENT

For maximum effect, also share a short video interview or written comment from the customer or client that they have provided at the end of the service or experience. Video interviews are always more powerful as they seem more credible and your audience can pick up on the tone, enthusiasm and authenticity of the interviewee. These should be recorded as soon as the service ends, not afterwards, wherever possible, as the process will be fresh in their minds. If written, this can be anonymous or not, it doesn't matter much, except that anonymous comments are more likely to be construed as "potentially fake".

Why this matters:

You're saying why you're brilliant without saying why you're brilliant! You're letting your customers do the talking. Anything they say about why you're brilliant will be even better received, because they appear impartial and objective.

Your potential clients will also naturally imagine themselves in the actual clients' shoes (so the closer your example can be to your ideal clients' scenario, the better). This leads them to feel more connected to what it's like to be your customer, and to have a clearer picture in their mind which usually moves them further along the sales cycle very naturally.

34

SHARE A SCREENSHOT OF A CLIENT MESSAGE OR EMAIL THANKING YOU FOR A BRILLIANT EXPERIENCE

Get in the habit of "screenshotting" or saving positive feedback in a shared folder — and encouraging any others within the company to do the same. You can then post these with a caption, for example, "Grateful for this feedback from one of our customers today!" Or "It was a pleasure to help Penelope with her {INSERT OUTCOME OF SERVICE} — thanks for taking the time to leave us a review Penelope!" Or "Thanks so much for sharing what it was like working with us Penelope!"

Why this matters:

First, it instils a warm, fuzzy feeling. If you missed it, I covered earlier in the book why warm, fuzzy feelings are good for your brand! (Hint: it's down to oxytocin and dopamine). It also creates a gratitude snowball. Your client is grateful, so you're grateful, and your audience are also more likely to feel that gratitude ripple too. Can you feel the gratitude glow already? :)

35

SHARE A SCREENSHOT OF A CLIENT MESSAGE OR EMAIL SHARING A SPECIFIC RESULT OR RESULTS THAT THEY ATTRIBUTE TO YOUR SERVICES

GET in the habit of saving or "screenshotting" client results and wins in a shared folder. Encourage everyone in the company to add to it. You can include a caption like "Celebrating {INSERT CLIENT'S NAME/COMPANY NAME} for these fantastic results {HE/THEY HAS/HAVE} seen after using our {INSERT SERVICE NAME}"

Or "Look at what one of our recent {INSERT SERVICE TYPE} clients achieved!". You can also include a call to action afterwards such as "To enquire about our {INSERT NAME OF SERVICE OR SERVICES}, just click the link below to schedule a call with one of the team."

Why this matters:

Evidence, evidence, evidence! These are evidence that you do what you say you do, that you do it well, and that it leads to results. Perception of results leads to greater confidence, which leads to greater willingness to spend (and to spend more), and a more positive working relationship from the get go.

36

TAKE A SNIPPET FROM A TESTIMONIAL OR REVIEW AND SHARE IT IN A VISUAL FORMAT

Use the most powerful snippet from a testimonial, put it into a nice graphic and post it, sharing how much you or your team enjoyed working with the client and how much you love what you do. Also, if you have, for example, an average 5* rating, include five stars at the bottom all filled in, to reinforce this. If the reviews are verified, also include the word "verified" and the number of reviews. E.g. "234 verified 5* reviews on {TripAdvisor/Facebook/Google etc}!"

Why this matters:

Reviews are received as tangible evidence of your efficacy. They occur as objective and impartial. They speak volumes, and most smart people can spot a fake review a mile off! Visual snippets are particularly eye catching and a great complement to other forms of content. When thrown into the mix with the other five Types of Content to Captivate and Convert, these are highly effective at generating new leads and sales, and faster.

37

SHARE A "BEFORE AND AFTER" CASE STUDY

SHARE a case study of where a client was before engaging you for your services, and where they are now. Make it as evocative as possible. What were they feeling, what were they doing, what were they not feeling and not doing? What felt hard or impossible or was taking too long? What now feels easy or possible or is happening smoothly and efficiently? Share in the following structure.

"When Betty from {INSERT COMPANY NAME IF YOU HAVE PERMISSION} came to us, she was really {INSERT NEGATIVE EMOTION} about {PROBLEM YOU HELP RESOLVE}. After using our {INSERT SERVICE NAME} she {AND HER TEAM, IF APPLICABLE} has/have seen {INSERT TANGIBLE OUTCOME(S)}. As a result of this, her/their {INSERT A SECONDARY TANGIBLE OUTCOME}, and she/they couldn't be happier with this result!"

This is the kind of content that should be used EVERYWHERE! On your social media channels, on your website, it can even go in your team's email signatures. Share it far and wide.

Why this matters:

It keeps your audience connected to the outcomes of your service or services. People rarely buy for the process, or for the journey (unless it's a trip!!); they buy for the outcome, first and foremost. A nice process or journey is usually secondary (and it's importance will vary depending on the customer). Outcomes first, everything else second.

These kind of case studies are incredibly effective at drumming up new business, and can also be really useful tools in the negotiation or objection handling stage of your sales process. They can be repurposed into both long-form and short-form content, for example glossy one page printable PDFs, but also 1-2 sentence summaries, like the example above.

38

CONDUCT A CUSTOMER/CLIENT INTERVIEW SERIES VIA VIDEO

Interview several clients, sharing their "before and after" stories in detail, in their own words. For the best results, you should interview a range of clients. For example, clients in different industries (if you serve different industries), or roles (if you serve clients in different roles) with similar but slightly different challenges, incomes or revenue levels and pain points.

Prepare some structured questions and ask each client the same questions. For best effects, livestream these videos and title them "Hear from our client {NAME} who went from {STARTING POINT} to {WHERE THEY ARE NOW} after {BUYING OUR X SERVICE / WORKING WITH US / INSERT OUTCOME OF WORK}.

Why this matters:

There's a time and a place for talking about why you're brilliant. And there's a time and a place for letting your customers and clients talk about why you're brilliant. This content achieves a double (or triple) whammy as it also makes your customers feel special *and* can give them exposure to your audience, which can be a great little bonus for their visibility and reach. These interviews can then be repurposed into shorter snippets too - see #39 for more on this!

39

TURN A LONGER INTERVIEW INTO SEVERAL PIECES OF SHORT-FORM CONTENT

TAKE one or more interviews mentioned in #38, and cut them up or have a team member cut them up into shorter pieces of content of anywhere between 10-60 seconds each. Make sure you add subtitles so that whether or not your audience are able to turn the sound on when watching, they still get the message!

Why this matters:

Not everyone will watch your long-form content. Some people are more drawn to long-form content, others don't have the patience for it. Presenting it in both forms gives you the chance to resonate with and get the message across to both types of people. Plus, different platforms favour shorter vs. longer-form content.

40

INTERVIEW A CLIENT AT AN EVENT

INTERVIEW A CLIENT AT A LIVE EVENT, meeting, conference or retreat that you've hosted and ask them what they got from the event. Be sure to include the event or meeting setting in the background to really bring it to life. Again ask specific questions.

Why this matters:

This creates FOMO, buzz and anticipation for your audience of what it might be like to also attend something you're hosting, and aligns it with the outcomes too. Bonus points if you then follow this with a call to action to join a waitlist or pre-book for your next conference or event!

41

ADD 5* RATED TO ALL YOUR CONTENT

If you have an average 5* rating from existing customer reviews, shout about it! Add it everywhere. Add it as a little icon on the edge of your images/social media templates, add it to the corner of your website, mention it in your call to actions. You can even add it to your email signature e.g., "Check out our 5* reviews here" (and link to the primary place where reviews have been left for you). If you do not have any or many reviews yet - ask for them. You can also incentivise them, for example, by offering to enter them into a prize draw to win something fun or to win a service (this can work particularly well if you have a passive or subscription service you can throw in!)

Why this matters:

You're reminding people that you're trusted. That they're in safe hands. That they don't have to worry and can get on with purchasing your services — and continuing to purchase them many years into the future, if they want to. Their purchases feel lower risk if "everyone else" is giving 5* ratings. If you don't yet have any ratings, or your average rating is below 5 stars, ask for more reviews first and once you do have a 5* rating, then apply the above.

42

ADD YOUR MOST IMPRESSIVE TESTIMONIAL TO YOUR COMPANY EMAIL SIGNATURE

PICK **one** testimonial that is particularly salient - for example, that pertains to the most common question or objection that you receive, and add it to your/your company email signature. You can also add it to landing pages, sales pages, your invoice footer etc. You can then rotate these over time if you wish, to keep things fresh.

Why this matters:

This is useful not only if you or members of your team are engaging in communication with potential customers, but it's also a great reminder for your existing customers. Feeling good about your company boosts retention and this is one of the little things that can contribute to that. Never underestimate the power of your testimonials!

43

INCORPORATE YOUR CLIENTS' WORDS INTO YOUR BIO/ABOUT PAGE

Be sure to use THEIR words, not yours! For example "Our clients call us {INSERT WHAT THEY CALL YOU THAT'S NICE}" or "My clients call me {e.g. THE KING/QUEEN OF X}". This can then be incorporated into your social media bios, your PR pitches, your sales pages and more.

Why this matters:

Anyone can appoint themselves the "King of the World", but when your customer says it? (Especially several.) Very different ball game. Whether or not your customers are ready to call you the King or Queen of the world(!), adding a turn of phrase you've heard from your customers or clients several times over really helps paint a bigger, brighter picture of your brand.

It also adds that extra layer of trust and prestige, especially if the words are from one or more particularly high-calibre clients and you have their permission to name them.

44

ADD CLIENT SNIPPETS INTO YOUR SALES VIDEO

If you have a sales video, add one or two snippets from your customer video testimonials here too. These can be written but video is best!

Why this matters:

This serves as additional evidence to support what you're saying in your sales video. It's a bit like "you've heard it from us - now hear it from our customers". You're providing an extra layer of credibility. This is especially true if the testimonials are from clients who are very high calibre, for example, partners of law firms, CEOs of major companies, and so on. Use your highest calibre testimonials here (that match or even exceed the calibre of the clients you're targeting) and watch your conversion rate soar!

45

CREATE A SERIES OF 1-PAGE PDF CASE STUDIES

CONDUCT short 10-15 minute interviews with 5-10 top customers, and turn them into a 1-page PDF case study each. Include a headshot of the customer, a short bio, and a deeper dive into their experience of your services. These can then be linked to in other content. For example, in a testimonial snippet you can include a call to action of "Read more in our brand new case study with customer Sarah from {CLIENT COMPANY NAME}" and then link to a hosted page with the PDF.

Why this matters:

You're building a bank of resources that show what's possible. That enables your potential clients to put themselves in the shoes of your case study clients and "test the water". Clients love case studies — especially very corporate and very risk averse clients! They can be great for getting budget owner/holder sign off or for use in pricing negotiations too. A chunky proposal or invoice suddenly doesn't seem so chunky in the context of an extraordinary case study that's directly relevant to your business type and size.

46

CREATE A VISUAL REPRESENTATION OF YOUR CLIENT TRANSFORMATION

TURN an example of a client transformation into a visual or graphic representation. For example, it might be a wheel, with where the client is when they come to you being in spoke 1, and where they end up after utilising your service being in the final spoke. It could be a flowchart. Or it could be a journey map or pathway. Map out the key steps in your clients' transformation and then turn it into a visual format and share it. You can include a caption like "Here's an example of what's possible when you become a {YOUR COMPANY NAME} client." Or "This is the journey we take our clients through at {COMPANY NAME}." This can then be used on many channels, and even in pitches and presentations too.

Why this matters:

Some people are learn and assimilate best through written or spoken stories. Others learn and assimilate best through images. Having a range of ways to reinforce a similar message helps appeal to different learning styles but also provides reinforcement and different ways of looking at the same benefits. This can cause something to "click" for your audience that might not otherwise click. These can also be very useful for conversations your client may need to have with a "budget owner/holder" as well.

Part Four

FACTS AND FIGURES

These are things like "did you know" statistics and numbers relevant to your zone of genius. For example, industry statistics, risks or costs associated with not using your services, or from getting it wrong, and indeed the quantitative benefits from getting it right with the help of your services.

47

SHARE A STATISTIC RELEVANT TO YOUR IDEAL CLIENT'S #1 PROBLEM OR CHALLENGE

This works especially well if it relates to a risk or challenge that is commonplace in your industry, that your expertise can help avoid. For example, "Did you know that 99% of potatoes don't know how to tie their shoelaces? This is why I do what I do!"

Or "Did you know 98% of {INSERT THEIR JOB TITLE E.G. ATTORNEYS} say they're drowning in {INSERT CHALLENGE, E.G. PAPERWORK / PHONE CALLS / ETC} and it holds them back from {THING THEY NEED TO SPEND MORE TIME ON E.G. BUSINESS DEVELOPMENT WORK}? This is why we created {INSERT SERVICE NAME}!"

Why this matters:

This format brings top of mind a problem or challenge that your ideal client has, that they may or may not have been hiding from or trying to pretend doesn't exist, and lets them know that a) they're not alone (this is more powerful than most service providers realise!), b) there's a way out and c) you specialise in helping them find the way out or resolve the problem.

The more shocking the statistic, the better! You want them to be thinking "wow, it's not just me" but also feeling the hunger to be the exception to the rule and SOON, thanks to your expert services.

48

SHARE A STATISTIC RELEVANT TO THE SUCCESS OF YOUR SERVICES

These statistics are usually best garnered through customer surveys which can be easily initiated using tools such as Typeform, SurveyGizmo etc. You ask your customers a set of questions such as "After signing up to {OUR SERVICES - INSERT TYPE OF SERVICE HERE} did you see an increase in {INSERT OUTCOME YOU HELP YOUR CLIENTS ACHIEVE}?"

Or "What % change did you see in {INSERT A METRIC HERE} after using our services?"

Or "How happy are you with our services on a scale of 1 to 10?" and so on.

This gives you some useful metrics that you can then use in this kind of content, e.g. "98% of our customers saw at least 50% increase in [THING THEY SEE AN INCREASE IN] after using our services."

Why this matters:

Just like testimonials, stats and figures put meat on the bones of what you say you stand for and can help with. They back up what you're saying and provide tangible proof that the benefits are real and measurable!

49

SHARE A STATISTIC OR FIGURE THAT INDICATES THE DANGER IF THEY DON'T TAKE ACTION

THIS COULD BE A PROJECTION, for example "Did you know it's anticipated that by {INSERT YEAR} 95% of jobs will be taken over by robots? If you want to stay relevant it's important to {INSERT ACTIVITY RELEVANT TO YOUR SERVICES}"

Or "Did you know {INSERT NUMBER OR PERCENTAGE} companies go bust every year because they're not legally protected and are swallowed up by the costs of avoidable litigation?". Whatever stats you share, make them relevant to the problem you solve.

Why this matters:

Humans are busy. Left to their own devices they will delay things that don't seem urgent or that they anticipate that, left unresolved, won't cause severely negative consequences. (Or not to their knowledge, at least.) With this kind of content, you are introducing the fact that there are dangers or risks associated with not taking action, that they may not have been aware of. This helps spur them into action. Avoidance of danger and pain is a powerful motivator! (Often even more powerful than positive outcomes.)

50

SHARE A STATISTIC OR FIGURE THAT SPEAKS TO WHAT'S POSSIBLE

THIS COULD BE SOMETHING LIKE, "{INSERT INDUSTRY NAME} is a {INSERT ROBUST FIGURE RE MARKET CAP SIZE e.g., £2.9 billion} industry. Or it could be "Did you know that you could save up to {INSERT AMOUNT OF TIME AS NUMBER OF HOURS OR A PERCENTAGE OF TIME} {INSERT ACTIVITY TYPE THAT YOU CAN HELP THEM SAVE TIME ON} by using {OUR SERVICES / INSERT NAME OF SERVICES}?". Or it could be something pertaining to a specific platform e.g. "Did you know that traffic on YouTube is up {INSERT PERCENTAGE} this year and traffic on {INSERT OTHER PLATFORM} is down by {INSERT OTHER PERCENTAGE} this year? Don't miss out on the opportunity to leverage this."

Why this matters:

You're contextualising any costs required to utilise the service with the benefits, opportunities and any savings that are available. It doesn't matter whether the savings are money, time, opportunity cost, or energy or mental load. These are all viable costs and benefits that are worth putting a number on. See #48 for more on how you can acquire some of these figures yourself. There may be other relevant and useful statistics already done by other organisations or research bodies too, relevant to the industry you're targeting and/or in - just make sure you credit whoever has done the research when mentioning these!

51

SHARE A CLIENT WIN THAT HAS A TIME VALUE

THIS MIGHT BE an amount of time saved or freed up for other activities. It could be an amount of time that a particular outcome (or task) took with the benefit of your services vs. without, as a direct point of comparison. You might have a few examples depending on company size or project type (time savings for an average smaller company client, vs. time savings for a larger corporate client, for example). These can be used for personal matters / B2C offerings too. Let's take the example of romance. How much time did they spend being single before they took your program and got into a fabulous relationship in a matter of months? Or weight - how much time did they spend not losing weight and feeling deflated before they took your program and lost it in a matter of months?

Why this matters:

Time is our most precious and only non-renewable resource. With this content you are directly tracking your services back to time. The higher calibre your clients, the more they value being able to "buy time back". Whether this is achieving an outcome over a shorter time frame, or having time immediately back in their pocket because it's taken off their hands... they value it. Be explicit about exactly how you might help them save time. And if you can't *guarantee* to save them time (because the outcome isn't that simple or predictable), make these simply examples of what's possible and include a disclaimer that timelines or amounts of time saved do vary depending on other factors.

52

SHARE A CLIENT WIN THAT HAS SOME KIND OF FINANCIAL VALUE

THIS MIGHT BE A REVENUE FIGURE, a profit figure, a percentage increase figure, a revenue per customer or lifetime customer value (LCV) figure. It might be a percentage of asset or net worth growth. Compile a range, and produce content round it. For example "Our client Sarah generated over {INSERT AMOUNT OF MONEY E.G. £100,000} extra revenue in just [INSERT TIME FRAME E.G. ONE YEAR} by using our {INSERT SERVICE NAME}. What would you do with an extra {INSERT AMOUNT OF MONEY E.G. £100,000 revenue}? To book a free trial just go to {INSERT LINK}" or "Our client Dave increased his {INSERT OUTCOME OR OUTCOMES, E.G. NET WORTH / SIZE OF ESTATE} by {INSERT PERCENTAGE OR AMOUNT] in just {INSERT TIME FRAME E.G. FIVE YEARS} by implementing [WHAT YOU HELPED HIM IMPLEMENT]".

Why this matters:

I want to give a caveat here to say that if you can't guarantee financial results, please please for your sake, for your customers' sakes, for your brand's sake, be clear that you can't guarantee financial results and that it depends on other external factors / individual efforts / market conditions, whatever else is relevant here. Once you've made sure you include the appropriate disclosures and/or disclaimers, sharing financial uplifts that your clients have seen as a result of using your services is a wonderful tool in client attraction, conversion and retention. At the end of the day, humans are reward-oriented, and money is one type of reward and result. One that changes lives and businesses for the better. Don't be afraid to speak to it.

Part Five

AUTHORITY BUILDING CONTENT

Authority-building content is things like standalone tips, advice and lessons relevant to your zone of genius and services. These will often be things that a person or company might be scared to share for fear of "giving it all away" but actually unless you're giving your actual services away, there isn't really such a thing. All other things being equal, the more authority building content there is out in the world from your brand, the better.

53

SHARE A BIT ABOUT YOUR EXPERIENCE AND CREDENTIALS

How many years have you or your team been doing what you do and what qualifies you or them to do it? What professional certifications do you/they have and who are these qualifications or certifications accredited by? Are there any other highly credible figures in your space who you or your team have learned from, studied with, or been mentored by?

Why this matters:

Your ideal clients want to feel confident and secure in your professional abilities and professional credentials are one way of predicting this (although not the only one!). As a service-based expert, being qualified, especially being highly qualified, increases the likelihood that whatever comes up (relevant to your zone of genius and services, of course), that you or your team will be equipped to help your ideal client with it, even if it involves recommending other services or add-ons that require additional costs etc.

If your ideal client is invested in receiving or achieving the outcome they want, then this provides an extra sense of peace of mind and security that they're in the right hands. You'll still want to be clear what their role is in the outcome, if any, but this can provide a lot of motivation and inspiration! With regards to other highly credible figures, if you have learned from, studied with or been mentored by these, and it is relevant to your ideal client (this will vary depending on your audience) this can be worth mentioning too, as it creates a Golden Halo Effect, whereby you are seen in an even better light because of being associated with the other person. So do it mindfully, and don't mention anyone's name who isn't highly credible and respected!

54

SHARE HOW MANY CLIENTS OR CUSTOMERS YOU / YOUR COMPANY HAVE ALREADY WORKED WITH OR SERVED

THIS DOESN'T NEED to be an exact figure. It can be "hundreds", "thousands", or indeed "millions", but do, of course, make it a truthful figure. The more specific, the better. For example "Over 500" is better, more evocative, and will appear more trustworthy than "hundreds". This can be number of individuals, number of companies, or both. You might also want to include numbers or percentages per industry, see #55 for more on this!

Why this matters:

Here you're contextualising the impact you or your company has already had, in terms of volume at least, and letting your ideal clients know that they're not going to be your "test runs". People don't mind being a "test run" / "beta client" / "practice client" for free or a heavily or sometimes even a slightly discounted rate, when they know in advance, but they don't want to be paying market rate *and* testing something brand new, as it won't feel like a fair exchange. This provides a sense of safety and reassurance that isn't going to be the case.

55

SHARE THE CALIBRE OF CLIENTS OR CUSTOMERS YOU'VE ALREADY SERVED

THIS CAN BE INDUSTRY SPECIFIC, positioned as a percentage of a specific niche. For example, "85% of magic circle law firms trust us with their {INSERT SERVICE TYPE/NAME}". Or it can be more vague, for example, "top global CEOs, celebrities and sports players trust {YOUR COMPANY NAME} with their {INSERT PROBLEM OR CHALLENGE YOU SOLVE}. The more specific the better.

Why this matters:

When you provide numbers contextualising your customer base, that are specifically relevant to your ideal clients' industry, especially the most highly respected portion of their industry, you create a sense of competitiveness. They naturally want to have what the most successful people or companies in their industry also have. There is a subconscious implication that if they have access to the same resources or services, they might also be in with a chance of achieving the same or similar level of success, if they want it. When it comes to celebrities and public figures, again, people love to know that they have what high profile people have, who may have many things that are not usually accessible to them. As you probably know, this is the foundation of much consumer advertising and why celebrities are so often featured in adverts! It's less relevant, however to B2B. Just make sure you're being truthful!

56

REMIND YOUR AUDIENCE OF YOUR OR YOUR TEAM'S CREDENTIALS AND THEIR PRACTICAL IMPLICATIONS

SHARE a reminder of the credentials you or your team have and lay it out incredibly simply. For example, "I'm certified and qualified in {INSERT THINGS YOU ARE CERTIFIED IN} by the {INSERT NAMES OF INSTITUTIONS THAT CERTIFIED YOU, INCLUDING CERTIFYING BODY/ACCREDITATION BODY IF THERE IS ONE}. This means that if you want to/are wanting help with {INSERT EXACT THINGS YOU HELP YOUR CLIENTS WITH, IN THE ABSOLUTE SIMPLEST TERMS POSSIBLE}, I can help you most effectively." You might also include here something like "So if you want the most up to date advice, based on the latest changes, trends and regulations, you've come to the right place."

Why this matters:

You're letting your clients know that you're not just the average expert who just rocked up on the street and decided to call themselves an expert. Your or your team's expertise is rooted in something, and it's verified and certified by someone other than just you! This is increasingly important in a world where false experts are popping up all the time, and with all the confidence and swagger of real ones, sometimes more!

57

WRITE A POST ABOUT A RECENT PROFESSIONAL DEVELOPMENT EXPERIENCE

SHARE a recent learning experience or training that broadened or deepened your expertise and will impress potential and existing clients. For example, "{I/OUR TEAM} recently took {INSERT NAME OF COURSE/PROGRAM ETC AND PROVIDER} in order to uplevel {MY/OUR - INSERT TYPE OF SKILL HIGHLY DESIRABLE TO YOUR IDEAL CLIENT}. {I/WE ARE} committed to continually expanding {MY/OUR} {INSERT YOUR TYPE OF EXPERTISE E.G. LEGAL / FINANCIAL / MARKETING, ETC.} expertise in order to better serve {MY/OUR} clients. {I/WE} are excited to bring this extra knowledge to all of {MY/OUR} private clients."

Bonus points if you follow this up with a call to action to book a personalised call with one of your team!

Why this matters:

The more that your ideal client is discerning and highly qualified themselves, the more they will seek services from other experts who are also highly qualified. Whilst, of course, it's possible to be brilliant at what you do without engaging in ongoing formal professional development, let's be frank — it's less likely. Sharing professional development experiences demonstrates that you are a person/company committed to continuous growth. This means your clients will be less concerned about whether you or your services might stagnate or lose relevancy or efficacy. Or about whether your expertise might be based on "old" rules or trends rather than current ones, or "what worked a decade ago", rather than what's working today. All of this feeds into their peace of mind and confidence in engaging you or your services.

58

SHARE A TIP RELEVANT TO A KEY PILLAR OF YOUR ZONE OF GENIUS

If you haven't already, it's a good idea to define your (or your brand's) expertise based on two or three key "pillars". I'm going to use me as an example here. I specialise in helping high-achieving, service-based experts to (1) attract, (2) convert and (3) retain more ideal clients.

Make the categories as simple and practical as possible. You might reference all three in a biography or introduction somewhere. Now share one key tip that's useful to your ideal client.

{INSERT A PIECE OF ADVICE OR KEY CONSIDERATION RELATING TO 1 OR MORE OF YOUR "PILLARS" HERE E.G. "DID YOU KNOW…?" OR SIMILAR}

Why this matters:

When you share tips in your free content, you're letting your audience know "hey, I care about you", "I want to help you, even if you don't pay me or haven't paid me yet". This builds trust and credibility deeply. They come to see you as someone they can rely on for valuable information, and they wonder "wow, if I can get this much value from [your name/your company's name]'s FREE content, I wonder how much more I can get when I actually pay them?". As a sidenote, it's a good idea to make sure that overall, no more than 20% of your content is a pure "pitch" or offer.

59

SOMEONE NEEDS TO HEAR THIS TODAY

NOT EVERYONE IS wild about these posts, but I really like them and get some of my best engagement on these. The idea is to put yourself firmly in your ideal clients' shoes, their challenges, their pain points, their desires and to ask yourself "what does my ideal client need to be reminded of today?" Or "what's one thing my ideal client would benefit from being reminded of today?". This can work particularly well when you're posting "in the moment" vs. pre-scheduling content as I believe if you are spiritually connected, these can so often be *exactly* what your followers needed to hear, in the exact moment they needed to hear it, even if your audience is huge! It can be a bit spooky actually, if you're new to this!!

Why this matters:

Done right, this can lead your ideal clients to almost feel like you are literally inside their heads. I can't tell you how many times ideal clients have said to me "Wow, this is EXACTLY what I needed to hear today, thank you so much!" And let's be clear - this doesn't have to be vague "could apply to anybody" statements. You're still only saying things that would apply to most or all of your ideal clients. You can also categorise these. For example "If you're a financial adviser, you might need to hear this today…" or "If you're a lawyer you might need to hear this today…" or "One for the ladies today.." etc. (This can work well if you have a personal brand and some of your work is very personal.) This both elevates your authority and your potential and actual clients' trust that you really "get" them.

60

RE-USE CONTENT FROM A RECENT PODCAST INTERVIEW

If you haven't already, do your research and find some podcasts your ideal client would (and does) listen to. Pitch to the podcast owner offering up a valuable conversation about a specific topic, and include a professional biography and links to any other podcast interviews you've done so they can get a sense for your style, if they want to. Once the podcast is done, take snippets from it, for example quote images or "audiograms" (short snippets of audio content with an image overlaid) and share these far and wide. Many podcasters will provide these as part of their process, but you might want to create your own too. Just be sure to credit the podcast and host and link back to the full episode!

Why this matters:

The wonderful thing about podcasts is not only do you have the opportunity to share your wisdom, but people also get to hear your voice and to feel your energy. The spoken word lands differently than the written word. The more aligned your energy is, the more magnetic your voice will be on audio and the more your ideal clients will want to connect with you. When you share your podcast interviews or excerpts from interviews you've done, you position yourself at a higher level. After all, who would interview someone who wasn't worth interviewing? You might even want to consider creating your own podcast, which can elevate your authority even more.

61

RUN A SUMMIT OR EVENT (AND RE-PURPOSE RECORDINGS FROM IT)

Running a summit or event, whether online or in-person, is a brilliant authority builder. The higher profile the other speakers and the more appealing they are to your ideal clients, the better. Done right, this can result in the "Golden Halo Effect" I mentioned earlier in the book. Just be sure that they share your values and positioning your name alongside theirs isn't going to backfire later down the line - especially if you're a person of high integrity!

Pick a theme that's salient to your ideal clients and make sure any other speakers know whether they can pitch or not (this is really important). If they can pitch, you'll likely want to agree a profit share. If they can't, they might still be allowed to share a free resource. It's all up to you. Then re-use snippets of recordings from the event both to promote future events and to affirm your authority.

Why this matters:

Re-using event content is great because you can make your audience feel like they were a fly on the wall at the event, even if they weren't there. You get to share the wisdom you shared at the event with a wider audience, and it automatically positions you at a higher level than just sharing the same content in afresh now (especially if it's video content). There is something about seeing you in front of an audience, whether in real life or virtually, that puts you in a different status. It also creates FOMO (fear of missing out) that can then help you sell more tickets or get more attendees at a future event. Share the absolute BEST bits of the event in terms of advice (especially yours!), but don't make it too long. Short snippets is best. Tag the other speakers in these posts and encourage them to re-share content too.

62

SHARE A THROWBACK THURSDAY TO AN EARLIER MOMENT THAT DEMONSTRATES AUTHORITY

Did you do a big talk a few years ago? Win an industry award? Publish a book? Share something really, really wise and get lots of engagement? Share it on a Thursday with a #TBT or Throwback Thursday. Mention how you felt at the time, including if you felt nervous, humbled, elated etc! Then tie it back to where you're at now. For example "Here's a snippet from my first talk {INSERT TIME AGO}, wow, I was so {INSERT EMOTION E.G. NERVOUS} back then!! Now I give talks every week. It's funny how things change isn't it? Grateful for the journey and to everyone who has come and listened to me speak!}

Why this matters:

When you do this, you're connecting your audience with the fact that you're not a flash in the pan. You've been here a while (perhaps many decades), and, God willing, you'll be here even longer still. You're not going anywhere.

When you share that you felt nervous or similar, you also humanise yourself. You subconsciously remind your audience that they don't need to feel 100% ready or 100% confident to do something amazing. This is a wonderful legacy to leave people with, whether or not they ever buy anything from you! (But hopefully they will buy from you too!)

Lastly, in this specific example, you're expressing gratitude for those who have invested their time and attention in listening to you. This is a lovely thing to do and may also prompt their memories, leading to positive comments from them recalling your talks too, reinforcing your authority even further.

63

RE-INTRODUCE YOURSELF

THIS MIGHT START with "Allow me to re-introduce myself" (usually followed by an announcement including a way in which you've recently changed, slightly pivoted etc.,) or a simple "Hello to those of you joining our little part of the internet" or "Hello, we're {BUSINESS NAME} and we stand for {THING YOU STAND FOR}"

Why this matters:

However you do it and whatever your unique brand voice, re-introducing yourself is a great thing to do. It reminds those who've followed you for a while what you stand for. And it ensures that those who are "new to your world" know exactly what is it you do. This all helps build authority from Day 1. We don't want people following your social media accounts for years thinking "oh yes, {he/she/INSERT COMPANY NAME posts} wise things. No idea what {he/she/INSERT COMPANY NAME does} though!". There's a time and a place for mystery in the world, and mystery about your authority isn't it!

64

GAMIFY YOUR EXPERTISE

This can include creating an actual game for people to play that creates extra engagement and interest, and affirms your expertise. Or it can include injecting fun into the little things you do. I once helped a tech brand create a game for developers to play. Developers love games. At the end of the game there were prizes, and a recap of current promotions. This worked well. It doesn't have to be an actual game though. It could be a prize draw linked to a new offering, e.g. "We just launched {NEW OFFERING} and to celebrate we're giving away {SERVICE YOU'RE GIVING AWAY}. To enter just tag two {INSERT TARGET AUDIENCE} in the comments. Prize draw closes {ENTER DATE IT CLOSES}". Or it could be creating a card deck, which I'll be doing with this book!!

Why this matters:

Gamification is smart because it can be used to capture new audience members, activate existing members and create new buzz and excitement around your brand. Your ideal client associating you with fun, even if just for a moment, will amplify how they engage with your brand long-term. Remember, we'll forget what you did, but we'll never forget how you made us feel! If this involves an actual game, just be careful it's not too complex or random, and that it aligns with your brand.

65

CREATE AN "ASK ME ANYTHING"

GIVE your followers the opportunity to ask you their any questions they've been wanting to ask you, then share the answers in your stories or a livestream.

You can always choose which questions to ask and which to not ask. Some might be fun and provide the opportunity to humanise your brand. Others should be directly relevant to your zone of genius. If you get totally random questions, your content needs refining, so do that and revisit this point later!

Why this matters:

You're sharing and affirming your expertise, firstly. It also shows that you're accessible, helpful and caring. People and brands who aren't helpful and don't care won't offer to answer questions for free. Just remember to give the appropriate disclaimers and/or disclosures if your advice depends on a range of other factors and unique circumstances etc. Answer the question or give advice to the extent you can based on the information provided, but also make it clear that you'd need to know more to give more in depth or tailored advice. This allows you to provide value, without completely substituting the need for your services or offerings or attracting endless freebie seekers. Also remember, you're not obligated to answer every single question if any irrelevant or inappropriate ones come through - you get to choose which ones to answer and not!

66

TURN YOUR TOP PERFORMING SOCIAL CONTENT INTO BLOG POSTS

TAKE your most highly engaged and commented on social media content and turn them into blog posts, podcast episodes, whatever you like!

Why this matters:

Your mostly highly engaged and commented on social media posts will tell you something about what your audience finds interesting. Dogs, children, weddings, new houses and new cars often perform best for personal brands, but don't build authority (though they can build connection, as mentioned in part one of this book), so don't make it about these unless it's directly relevant to your niche. (Also note, new car photos are getting a bit old / cliche now online!)

Look at your social media content sharing your *expertise*, what is highest performing, and turn it into content for other mediums. Blog posts, guest expert blog posts, podcast episodes (on your podcast or someone else's), are all possibilities. This gives you the chance to expand further on topics you already know your audience are interested in. Just remember, it's possible that not all of your audience are ideal clients, so always run this through the filter of "would my ideal client find this valuable and insightful?" as well. For guest expert blog posts, approach blogs that are directly relevant to your niche and that your ideal client would potentially visit.

67

CREATE AUDIOGRAMS OR VIDEO SNIPPETS FROM YOUR OWN PODCAST, GROUP TRAININGS OR COURSES ETC

Whether you have a podcast, deliver group trainings or talks, or have online courses, this will be of use. I mentioned using audiograms from other people's podcasts in a previous tip, but this is different when it's *your* podcast or program. You might take a 60 second snippet from a recent training you delivered or a talk you did, add subtitles to it and then include a call to action. (For example, to find out more about the course, your next event, your group training programs etc.) Just pick one call to action and use the audiogram to increase engagement and conversions from it.

Why this matters:

Nothing quite beats giving your audience the opportunity to actually experience and witness your expertise and wisdom first hand. It could be a conversation with a singular client (with consent), a recording of a group training, or any of the other options above, but make it count and make it salient! Pick something that's a question you get ALL the time from potential clients or actual clients and make it pop. For example a big header that says "How do I {INSERT QUESTION}?" and then add subtitles and a juicy caption.

Tip: make sure it's in your terms and conditions that you record all events and by attending, participants are giving consent to event recordings being shared.

68

SHARE MENTIONS FROM OTHER AUTHORITATIVE PEOPLE OR BODIES

If another person or brand mentions you and they're well-respected by your ideal clients, share it. They might write a nice comment, mention you in a post or they might say something verbally. Get their permission to share it and then either screenshot or quote verbatim. For maximum effect, combine this with a photo of you or your CEO with the person in question as this really brings it to life as well as being more memorable.

Why this matters:

The more you associate yourself with others who are well-respected and credible, the more your clients and potential clients will assume that you're also worthy of the same, since birds of a feather tend to flock together. Unless they've gone off the rails (it happens), people who are well-respected and credible don't tend to like to be seen or to associate their names with those who are not, so by the process of elimination this increases the perception that you're probably not awful. This helps boost your authority.

By the way, this doesn't mean turning into a fan girl/boy who takes a photo with every high-profile person they meet and writes a long post about it — this can actually diminish your authority rather than elevate it as you're positioning yourself beneath others. But rather, it means leveraging the relationships you already have and are already making in a smart way. This can be a total win-win too, as when you do this, as long as you're credible yourself, you're also reinforcing their brand too. Everyone's a winner!

69

SHARE YOUR AWARDS

THIS COULD BE a picture of all of your or your company's physical awards on a shelf, or it could be a picture with you or one of the team with one particular award. If you're award-winning, shout about it!

Why this matters:

Award-winning indicates an external or "objective" validation of your authority. It adds prestige. You worked to get the award, now milk it!! I have an important caveat here: be mindful that some awards are purely "pay to play". I strongly recommend avoiding these as it defeats the whole object - you didn't actually "win" or "earn" an award at all if all you had to do was pay for it! Even if an application (or nomination) is required to be eligible for winning an award, the judging process can still be fair. Only associate yourself with — or put yourself or your company forward for — awards that are credible. This doesn't mean don't pay to get greater publicity - for example, there are many credible awards where you can pay extra to get a boosting to your listing that you already earned or a physical trophy. This can be a sensible thing to do, but only if it's a credible award and awarding body. I think I've said my piece here! :)

70

GET SOME PR

TAKE your zone of genius and your best-performing content and come up with some angles for PR. Then pitch (or have someone in your team or an external PR expert pitch) these ideas to major and/or industry publications.

Why this matters:

The more you can be appearing in national, international, and/or industry publications, the better. It's sad that there are people who aren't actually very good at what they do, who get some good PR and people assume they are great and then it all ends in tears. The phrase "sex, lies and PR" isn't a phrase for nothing. But PR can absolutely be used for good. Just because not everyone who uses it is good, doesn't mean *you* can't use it for good. Again, like with awards, just be mindful of the publications you choose to associate yourself with. You might have to start small as you build up your "bank" of PR (not necessarily though!), but nothing fishy!!

71

SHARE A COMMON QUESTION THAT'S RELEVANT TO YOUR IDEAL CLIENT, AND ANSWER IT

TAKE a question you hear all the time from potential clients and actual clients, and answer it. It might be in written format or video format. It really doesn't matter. Just get it out there! Answer it as simply and clearly as possible, and include a call to action if relevant. For example, if you've written a blog post, or a free guide that delves into this topic further, or if it's one of the topics you cover in a program, mention that too.

Why this matters:

Firstly, you're leveraging the power of curiosity. Who wants to see a question and not see the answer?! Secondly, you're showing your authority in a highly practical, clear, and demonstrable way. Never underestimate the power of just answering your ideal clients questions or giving them a preview of your actual expertise or guidance. There is no marketing quite like it. Just don't give away "too much" of the answer. Leave them hungry for more!

72

CREATE A MEME ABOUT A KEY CHALLENGE YOUR IDEAL CLIENT MIGHT BE FACING

TAKE a challenge or blocker you hear about all the time from your clients and ideal clients and turn it into a funny picture or video and tie it back to your brand. For example, "Bob had enough {INSERT CUSTOMER CHALLENGE. E.G. "THE PRINTER NOT WORKING"}. It was time to call {INSERT YOUR COMPANY NAME}." This is a terrible example, but you get the point!!

Here's another one: "Peter had been up all night working when he realised, all he actually needed to do was sign up to [INSERT YOUR BRAND NAME + SERVICE NAME]". Make the image dramatic and/or comical.

Why this matters:

You're demonstrating a sense of humour *and* a deep understanding of your ideal client all at once. This is highly magnetic and compelling. Plus, who couldn't do with a laugh? No matter how corporate your brand is, at least some funny content is always a bonus.

73

CLARIFY A MISUNDERSTOOD INDUSTRY TERM OR MYTH

CLARIFY A MISUNDERSTOOD INDUSTRY **term or myth**

Take an oft-misunderstood situation, term or industry myth and debunk it! (See tips #69 and #70 and notice how I've done this here with awards and PR — people assume that awards and PR coverage are *always* good signs — but this isn't actually the case!)

Why this matters:

When you're willing to clarify muddy waters or speak up about something that doesn't work, it creates much deeper trust. That you're not just an authority but that you're an authority with standards, values, and morals. To the right clients, this is really appealing. It also shows that you don't sway with the wind. You're anchored. You're grounded. You stand for something! If your ideal clients are the same, you're onto a winner.

74

SHARE A RELEVANT INDUSTRY ARTICLE/NEWS

TAKE a recent industry happening or trend, and share an authoritative article about it. Bonus points if it's a high-profile or highly regarded industry publication.

Why this matters:

This shows you're up to date on current trends. It also aligns you with the credibility and name of the publication you're sharing. Customers and clients want to work with businesses that know what they're doing and that know what's happening relevant to their zone of genius. It tends to make you better at optimising your offerings and helping your customers get better results. Just don't go overboard, too much sharing of other people's or other company's content can actually deposition you and your brand.

Part Six

OFFERS

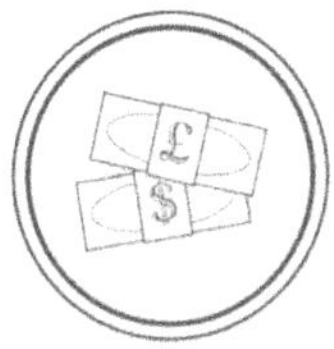

This is the piece many forget! The other categories of content are all very well, but if you aren't making offers regarding your services, how will your ideal clients know what and how to buy from you? Don't forget this piece! This includes: reminding your followers about your services, including links to buy new or existing services, making time-limited promotional offers, offering free trials, and more.

Important note: make offer content no more than 20% of your content, unless it's as a "P.S." to a longer piece of genuinely useful/insightful content, or you run the risk of annoying your audience and causing them to disengage.

If you are including at least some of your offers as a "P.S." which is added to the end of valuable free content (as prompted in a few earlier examples in this book), you can make this percentage higher.

I also want to mention here, action words such as "like", "comment", "share", etc., can be very useful for boosting engagement, but they aren't offers. Offers are where you are inviting a potential or current client to download, register, buy or enquire about a specific product or service — whether free or paid. These and these alone are offers.

75

SHARE A FREE RESOURCE

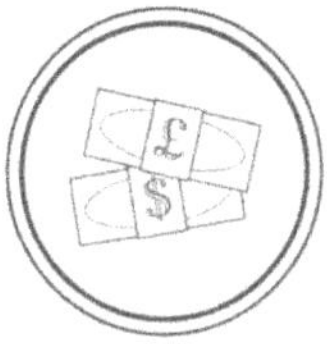

SHARE a free resource such as a guide, toolkit, or sample in exchange for an email address or postal address. "Have you downloaded my {INSERT NAME OF FREE RESOURCE HERE} yet? If you haven't and you want to {INSERT OUTCOME THE RESOURCE WILL HELP THEM ACHIEVE}, grab it here: {INSERT LINK}."

Why this matters:

You're putting your money where your mouth is and saying "I believe in our value so much that I'm going to give you something free to prove it to you". You're saying "I'm not going to ask for anything, I want to show you the value first." You're also letting them reduce the risk. You're not asking them to jump straight into bed with you. You're letting them take their time. This makes them feel more safe with you and your brand, and more likely to buy later if your services are a good fit.

Just make sure this is all linked up to a funnel where, in registering for the free resource, they also receive further emails letting them know more about you and an opportunity to buy the "next natural step" in your offers afterwards. You earned it by sharing the free resource!!

76

SHARE A FREE TRIAL OFFER THAT YOU HAVE

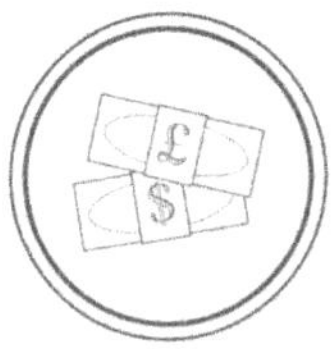

It blows my mind how many companies don't have a free trial offer, or who don't talk about it nearly enough in their content! A free trial, especially for anything that has little to no "set up" cost or cost of delivery for you as a service provider is a no-brainer. Even if there is a set up cost, it's often still a no-brainer, as long as you have a good conversion rate of customers staying after the trial.

Just be aware that some people are gross and will take a free trial to try and download your entire library of resources or content and then cancel, so it's a good idea to put something in place to help prevent or avoid this. (For example a limit to the downloads possible during a trial, if it involves online resources.)

Here's one way you can talk about this: "Did you know we offer a 14-day trial of our {INSERT SERVICE NAME}? No? You do now! Click this link to set one up today: {INSERT LINK}"

Why this matters:

Like with sharing a free resource, you're giving your customer the opportunity to try before they buy. Two things usually happen here. If they're a genuinely ideal client with the challenges or goals that you help solve, and they aren't stuck in the "so busy they need you but also so busy they don't have time to actually use the service" cycle, they will get hooked.

Further, if you have taken their card details (which I always recommend — this is a very fair exchange for offering a free trial) — depending on the cost of the service, most people will forget to cancel. Once they've paid they're then even more likely to engage with the service in order to get their money's worth, which means they're more likely to reap the rewards, and then to stay.

It's really, really important if you do take card details, however, that you make it easy for people to cancel — it's incredibly icky when businesses have free trials that are then almost impossible to cancel — practically forcing you to pay them. But free trials used properly are a great tool! And it's totally fine to offer a free trial without taking card details too. It's very much up to you and your brand.

77

SHARE A FREE LIVE EXPERIENCE OR CHALLENGE

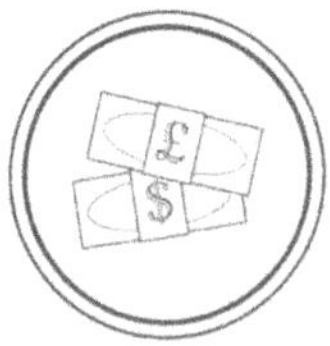

RUNNING a free live taster experience or challenge can be a brilliant way to drive extra leads for your services. A 3-4 day online experience with a short live training, Q&A or other free resource provided daily tends to be best. Any more than 3-4 days and people will drop off rapidly (same if the content is pre-recorded vs. live). Your post about this might be "I've got a free 4-day challenge coming up to teach you how to {INSERT THING YOU HELP YOUR CLIENTS WITH}] and I'd love to see you there. We start on {INSERT DATE YOU START ON}, just click the link below to save your space.

Why this matters:

These are perfect for creating buzz and getting new *and* existing clients re-engaged. Don't panic if existing clients sign up — they'll likely benefit from the reminders too, and they'll be some of your best brand ambassadors! Make sure to encourage your audience and customers to invite their friends or colleagues too, and you can incentivise this if you want. For example, you might have prizes inside for participation, on a prize draw basis, and there might be a prize for the person who invites the most people too. Just make sure you mention that there's a prize draw in your content (and exactly what they could win!) as this can really boost sign ups! These are such a win-win as they enable your potential customers to get to know you better, they can create a lot of buzz, and they also help repel non-ideal clients who you don't want to buy from you. You might then charge for this content after the designated time frame, if you wish.

78

SHARE AN EXCLUSIVE OR TIME-LIMITED PROMOTIONAL CODE

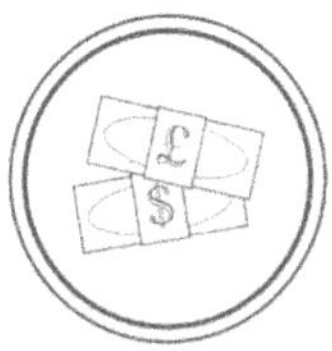

SHARE an exclusive or time-limited discount or promotional code. This can be a great thing to do around "Black Friday", "Cyber Monday" for example, but also Christmas, New Year, or your company anniversary. Or really any time you are wanting to boost sales and reward your customers!

"Get 20% off a subscription to {INSERT SERVICE NAME} by entering promo code {ENTER PROMO CODE HERE}, valid until {INSERT EXPIRY DATE}"

Why this matters:

With a time-limited offer or promo code, you're specifically firing off your potential clients and/or clients reward systems in their brains, so do use these ethically! You don't want a potential client signing up just because of a promotion, if your services aren't actually a good fit for them and they're going to be difficult or impossible for you or your team to service, or are going to end up leaving a bad review!

That being said, promotional codes can be a wonderful way of rewarding your audience for sticking with you. It makes them feel special and validated for their loyalty in following you online, even if they haven't bought from you before. Of course, these can also work particularly well with existing customers who already love your services, and a promo code simply encourages them to make their next purchase sooner rather than later. This can also be linked to customer survey if you wish, for example, if they answer your customer survey, they receive the promotional code as a thank you.

79

SHARE A PAID OFFER THAT YOU HAVE THAT'S LOW-ENTRY

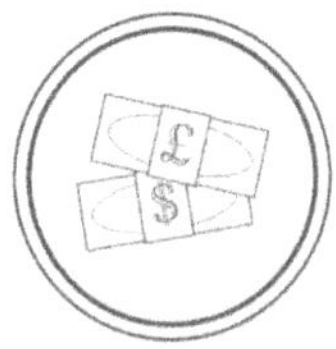

SHARE a low-entry paid offer that you haven't shared about yet or haven't shared about recently. For example "Did you know about {INSERT SERVICE OR PROGRAM NAME} you can get started for just {INSERT PRICE + TIME FRAME E.G. £92 PER MONTH}, even if you're not ready for our higher level services yet. Don't wait to get the support you need!"

Why this matters:

You never know who might not be ready to buy your higher-level services, but who would with DELIGHT in investing £49, £99 or similar in a low-entry offer. If you don't have a low-entry offer you'll be missing out on a lot of extra sales. It's also a myth that people will buy a low-entry offer instead of a high-ticket one. Those who want (and can truly afford) high-ticket will usually buy high-ticket. You're just capturing more of the market with a low-entry offer. It's rare that this will actually cannibalise your higher ticket offers unless it's the exact same or a very similar thing that they're receiving! As long as your offers are sufficiently differentiated, trust the process.

80

SHARE A PAID OFFER THAT YOU HAVE THAT'S MEDIUM-TIER

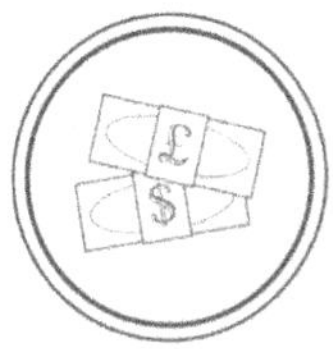

For example, "Did you know we offer three levels of service, depending on where you are/depending on your needs? {INSERT BRIEF SUMMARY OF THE THREE OR MORE LEVELS OF SERVICE}. {INSERT NAME OF MEDIUM TIER SERVICE} is currently open, click here to learn more: {INSERT LINK}."

Why this matters:

It's important to share offers at all different levels. Depending on where a potential client is at will affect how much they're ready and willing to invest and which solution they will therefore want to benefit from. This can include where they are at financially, but also the amount of time they are willing or able to devote to utilising the service or services, current workload, current goals and other external and/or personal factors.

Promoting a medium tier offers or offers as well as high and low-ticket or tier offers is important because it enables you to meet your ideal clients where they're at and to capture more market share. You're helping to avoid an "all or nothing" purchasing scenario where they're either "all in" or they're buying from another provider. You're enabling them to stay with you for more (or perhaps all) of their journey. This tends to help increase LCV (lifetime customer value) significantly.

81

SHARE A PAID OFFER THAT YOU HAVE THAT'S HIGH-TIER

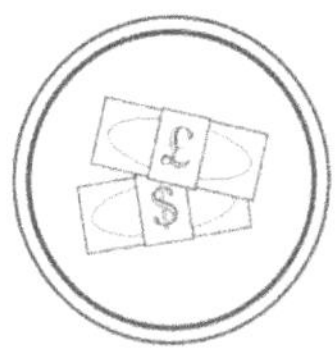

REMIND your audience of your high-tier or high ticket offering. You might think that it's not worth mentioning this publicly, that it's best to only mention it to existing contacts or previous buyers. This isn't true. Whilst the majority of customers will buy a lower level offer first, and work their way up the "ladder", there are "unicorns" that exist who will go straight in at your higher level offering. This will be particularly true if you've ticked all six types of content shared in this book, and also if they are particularly time pressured and/or keen to attain the result or have the problem solved that you help with as a matter of urgency.

You might say something like "Did you know, for those customers who want to {INSERT OUTCOME YOU HELP YOUR CLIENTS ACHIEVE} in the shortest time possible, we offer {INSERT NAME OF HIGHEST LEVEL OFFERING}? Click here to learn more: {INSERT LINK}". You can replace this with a link to book a call, if the offering is completely personalised and therefore a sales page doesn't exist.

Why this matters:

Never underestimate the impact of sharing your highest tier offer! I see so many experts not sharing their highest tier offer in their content because they think they should only share free or low cost offers publicly. This isn't true. Share them all! Just don't share them all every single day. Only in this situation can you confused your potential clients and you know what a confused mind says! (No!) You never know who in your audience who has never bought before is ready and ripe to purchase your highest level offering. And they can't buy what they don't know exists.

82

SHARE ALL OF YOUR PAID OFFERINGS IN ONE "WAYS TO WORK WITH ME" POST

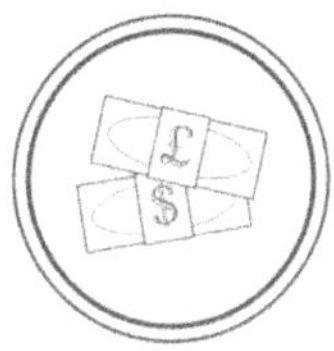

CREATE a post summarising very briefly the different services you have and ideally including pricing as well (if it varies depending on other factors, include a price range). A great format for this can be an infographic such as a pyramid or a ladder. There's no reason for such a graphic to be "internal only" unless it's messy! Create a nice, clean, clear, customer-facing visual summary of your paid offerings and share it.

"If you want to {INSERT OUTCOMES YOU HELP WITH}, here's a reminder of the different ways you can work with us, wherever you're at. Send us a message to enquire further."

Why this matters:

This creates total transparency regarding your offerings (especially if pricing or price ranges are shown in the image) and also lets your ideal clients know that there are a range of ways to benefit from your expertise. It lets your audience know that becoming a paying customer or client doesn't need to be "all or nothing". What tends to then happen is you then capture more of the market share, and you're also constantly creating leads for your higher-level offerings from customers who have joined the lower parts of the pyramid* or ladder and got hooked!

(*Note, I said pyramid not pyramid scheme!!)

83

SHARE A LOW-TICKET EVENT YOU'RE HOSTING

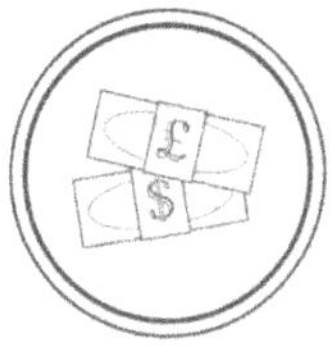

HAVE a virtual or in-person event coming up? Share it! KISS - keep it simple stupid. (I'm not calling you stupid, this acronym is just a great reminder to simplify simplify simplify!!)

"Did you know I/we have an event coming up on {INSERT DATE OF EVENT}, where we're going to be working on {INSERT OUTCOMES YOU HELP YOUR IDEAL CLIENTS ACHIEVE}". Just click the link below to save your space."

Or "Did you know I/we have an event coming up on {INSERT DATE OF EVENT}, where you can come along and learn how to {INSERT WHAT THEY'LL LEARN AT THE EVENT}. Just click the link below to save your space."

Why this matters:

Never assume that your audience know about your upcoming events or are clicking on your "event" page if you have one on your website. Share about your events and share often. At least 1-3 months before an event (longer if you're expecting people to travel from far and wide), and then multiple times again as you get closer to the event date. You can also prompt them to join a specific mailing list if you have one just for upcoming events. Customers who have had an in-person experience with your or your brand — even a low-ticket experience — are also much more likely to buy further services as all being well, they will feel closer to your brand after "real life" interaction. This is why so many businesses will happily create low-ticket events that are loss-leaders. The value is in the upsell and the LCV (lifetime customer journey)!

84

SHARE A HIGH-TICKET EVENT YOU'RE HOSTING

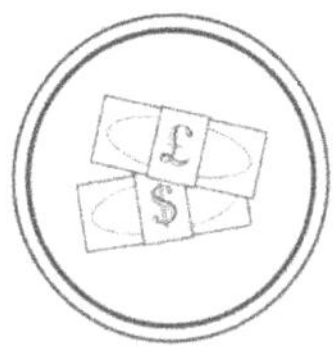

HAVE A HIGHER ticket event coming up? Share it!!

"Did you know I/we have an event coming up on {INSERT DATE OF EVENT}, where we're going to be working on {INSERT OUTCOMES YOU HELP YOUR IDEAL CLIENTS ACHIEVE}". Just click the link below to save your space."

Or "Did you know I/we have an event coming up on {INSERT DATE OF EVENT}, where you can come along and learn how to {INSERT WHAT THEY'LL LEARN AT THE EVENT}. Just click the link below to save your space."

Why this matters:

As per #83, never assume that your audience know about your upcoming events or are clicking on your "event" page if you have one on your website. Share about your events and share often. At least 1-3 months before an event (longer if you're expecting people to travel from far and wide), and then multiple times again as you get closer to the event date.

You can also prompt them to join a specific mailing list if you have one just for upcoming events.

Remember, customers who have had an in-person experience with your or your brand are much more likely to buy further services as all being well, they will feel closer to your brand after "real life" interaction. Again, also remember that there are "unicorns" who will go from never having bought a single service to purchasing a high-ticket offering very quickly, as long as they trust you and are hungry to get the result you can help with ASAP. Don't be surprised if you get more "unicorns" popping up after implementing this content. As I said earlier, they can only buy what they know exists!

85

SHARE YOUR REFERRAL PROGRAM

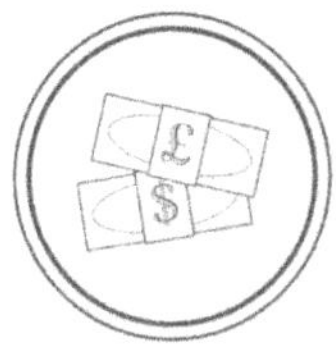

THE CLEANEST WAY TO do this is to have a "refer a friend" hub or page on your website, where your customers or clients can either a) create a custom referral link that tracks back to their account or b) enter a friend or colleague's email address and send an automated invite that will track back to them. There are ways to do this manually instead, for example having them send a personal email making an introduction, but obviously this isn't very scaleable!

You might say "Did you know we operate a referral program that gives you [INSERT CASH OR VOUCHER AMOUNT OR NAME OF GIFT OR PERCENTAGE COMMISSION} when you refer a friend or colleague? Click here to learn more: {INSERT LINK HERE}."

Another option is "Tag a friend and receive a code for {INSERT PERCENTAGE} off all services. Offer expires {INSERT DATE OFFER EXPIRES}". However these require a lot more manual input to manage so I really don't recommend them.

Why this matters:

You can attract a LOT of extra potential clients and purchases from setting up and sharing a robust referral program! Who better to know other ideal clients than your existing ideal clients and audience? Let them do the hard work for you. They'll also become more invested in the brand as we tend to like those we help more. Interesting, huh?

86

SHARE A PRIZE DRAW

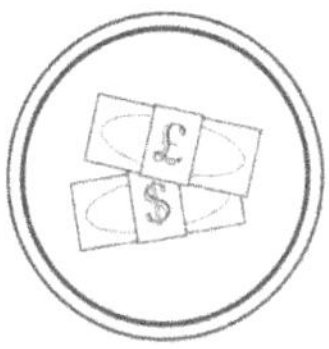

THIS COULD BE a prize draw for buying during a particular time frame or for taking a particular action, but create an epic prize draw and shout about it.

"Did you know, if you sign up to {SERVICE NAME} this week you'll be entered into a prize draw to win {INSERT PRIZE}. To sign up, just go here {LINK}"

Why this matters:

Prizes are fun. We are more inclined to take action on something we've been wanting to do anyway if there's a potential prize involved. Especially if it's something we love the sound of or have been wishing about! Make it a prize your ideal client will LOVE, ideally something they can hold in their hands from a brand of a similar calibre to yours, or something experiential pertaining to your own brand, for example a complimentary service or similar.

Your audience might be entered for making a purchase, for tagging a friend, the criteria is up to you. But the more automated the draw the better, otherwise this can be a real faff if you have a huge audience. One thing's for sure though, if it's a good prize, they won't forget about it in a hurry!

87

SHARE A SALE

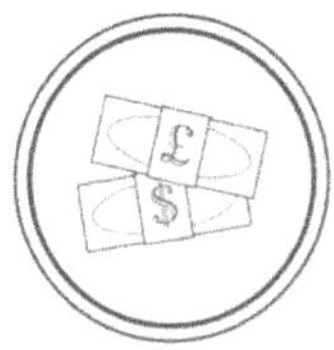

Human beings love a sale - need I say more?! Here's an example of what you might say:

"Our {INSERT OCCASION} sale is here until {INSERT DATE SALE ENDS}. Find out more and take advantage of up to {INSERT POTENTIAL SAVINGS AS A % OR £ VALUE} here: {INSERT LINK}."

Why this matters:

Humans love feeling like they've got a special deal - even though they might actually be spending more than they otherwise would, it makes them feel like they've got money back in their pocket. A sale can create a lot of extra buzz and purchases. Just make sure you're not running or promoting too many sales or too often— especially for anything that involves a live service vs. for example a service that doesn't have a cost of delivery — or you can inadvertently devalue and deposition your brand. Make sure there's always a clear reason too. For example, to reward your loyal customers, to give back/say thank you for sticking with you on your business birthday, because you have a sale "every October" or "special prices" on services "every Monday" etc. Make sure it makes sense to you and to your customers and they aren't thinking you're just putting on a sale because you're in a muddle. Make sure they feel excited and special!

88

SHARE A COLLABORATIVE OFFER

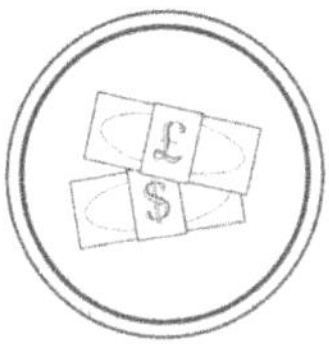

THIS COULD BE TAKING part in a collaborative bundle sale of online resources from a range of your peers. (These are quite common online). It could be creating a bundle offer of services with a local brick and mortar business that offers complementary but non-competing services that expands both of your reach. Or it could be creating an exclusive offer that is only available to customers of another business where you offer their customers an offer and they offer your customers an offer. This can be a very filial thing to do and is a great idea if you both have the same ideal clients.

You would post about the other business, and the other business would post about you, for example "Did you know that as a customer of {INSERT YOUR BUSINESS NAME} you can benefit from an exclusive {INSERT PROMOTION AMOUNT AS A % OR £ AMOUNT} off services at {INSERT OTHER BUSINESS'S NAME}, just mention {INSERT YOUR BUSINESS NAME} when booking."

(The alternative is to provide a custom link, if you have very large amounts of traffic.)

Why this matters:

You're creating an alliance with another business or businesses with the same target market but non-competitive services. The more businesses that are part of this, the more each individual business has the potential to grow their audience and reach new ideal clients.

In this instance, you usually aren't worried about affiliate income or commission, you're doing it to expand your reach. This can be a huge win-win for everyone - more ideal clients discover you, more ideal clients discover complementary services, you get to support other businesses that you share values with. It's a triple whammy!

89

COUNTDOWN TO A NEW OFFERING

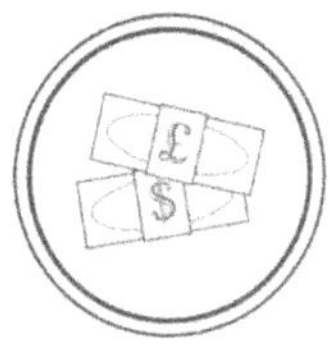

You're launching a brand new service or offering, you and your team have put so much work into it, maybe you've beta tested it and got customer feedback, refined it, and now it's ready to go!

Don't just put it out there all of a sudden from nowhere. Create some suspense and mystery! Do a mystery countdown, letting your audience know that something new is coming and you're very excited. You might reveal one piece of information or detail about the new offering each day over, for example a 7-14 day countdown, such that it becomes clearer the closer you get to the "drop date". Or you might create some kind of "puzzle" image where a small part of the image is revealed each day of the countdown until the image becomes completely clear.

"We are so excited to reveal our brand new proprietary {INSERT SUITABLY VAGUE DESCRIPTION OF SERVICE} in just a few days now. Can you guess what it is yet?"

Why this matters:

However you do it, this is a wonderful way to create anticipation around a brand new offering. It creates a mystical, almost childlike curiosity and excitement for all involved. It is a form of gamification.

Have you ever been to one of those "prohibition style" bars where the entrance is hidden and it's all mysterious, then you push a buzzer and give a code word and then you enter through one door and then another door and then perhaps through a turning bookcase or a spiral staircase and then you're finally there. And even though the prohibition era is long gone, it just feels so special and exciting!

Just because you're running a serious business, doesn't mean you can't create moments of pure delight and excitement for your customers. The more memorable (in a good way) the better.

90

AFFILIATE FOR OTHERS WITH THE SAME IDEAL CLIENT BUT DIFFERENT, COMPLEMENTARY OFFERINGS

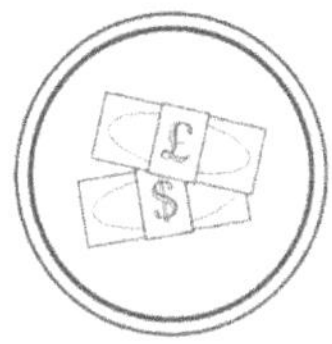

Affiliating for other businesses with different (but complementary) services to yours, and the same ideal client, can be a really wonderful way of being rewarded for the credibility and trust that you have worked so hard to gain from your audience, and for making a valued connection and introduction between your audience and other "partner" services that they can benefit from.

You might choose to only affiliate where there is a mutual (i.e. two-way affiliate relationship) or you may choose to affiliate simply because you are a big fan of the other business's (or businesses') services, you share the same values and you know your both of your clients will benefit tremendously. Only do this when you would gladly recommend the other offerings even if you weren't being compensated. This helps preserve the integrity of your brand. In addition, don't promote affiliate offers too close to your own offers as this can potentially cannibalise your own offers.

A post regarding this might look like "Did you know {INSERT NAME OF OTHER BUSINESS}'s {INSERT NAME OF/BRIEF DESCRIPTOR OF THEIR SERVICES} are the perfect complement to our {INSERT NAME/BRIEF DESCRIPTOR OF YOUR SERVICES}. Many of our customers use both in tandem and see incredible results. Click here to learn more: {INSERT AFFILIATE LINK}"

Why this matters:

By promoting the offerings of businesses providing different but complementary services to yours, you are amplifying your status as a trusted advisor to your clients. Just don't over-do it. Too much affiliating can actually diminish your own brand.

Also, if the way that their services and your services complement each other is complex or there is some kind of technical integration required, make sure this is detailed on your affiliate link. Make it clear why this makes sense and what the benefits are, plus any special added bonuses that are only available when using your partner link.

AFTERWORD

That's our 90 days of content ideas to captivate and convert your ideal clients done!

Did you find them useful?

If you liked this book, please share it. Let's grow and support each other to create better content and more magnetic brands online. Don't forget to also register for your exclusive book bonuses at www.jaimiesarah.com/content-bonuses. You'll then be added to my newsletter too so we can stay in touch!

Finally, I'd love for you to post a picture of yourself with your copy of the book, I love seeing your pictures! I'm on Instagram at @definitely_definitely and my other links are below. Make sure to use the hashtag **#90daysofcontent** too!

WORK WITH ME

I hope you enjoyed this book and I can't wait to hear how you get on implementing some of these ideas! If you want to share a win you've had from using them, please feel free to email me at hello@jaimiesarah.com or tag me on social media.

Instagram: www.instagram.com/definitely_definitely

Facebook: www.facebook.com/definitelydefinitely

LinkedIn: www.linkedin.com/in/jaimiesarah

Feel free to include the hashtag #90daysofcontent when you're using the tips so I can see the great things you're creating and cheer you on!

To get your free book bonuses, just go to;

www.jaimiesarah.com/content-bonuses

To work with me further, check out my website www.-jaimiesarah.com where you can learn about other ways I can help you and your brand become more magnetic to the exact customers you want to become more magnetic to, through super aligned energy, messaging and offerings.

I run a wonderful low-cost membership, a close-knit mastermind, and I also provide 1-1 consulting and "done for you" agency services.

I look forward to connecting with you and supporting you further very soon.

Jaimie

ABOUT THE AUTHOR

Jaimie Sarah

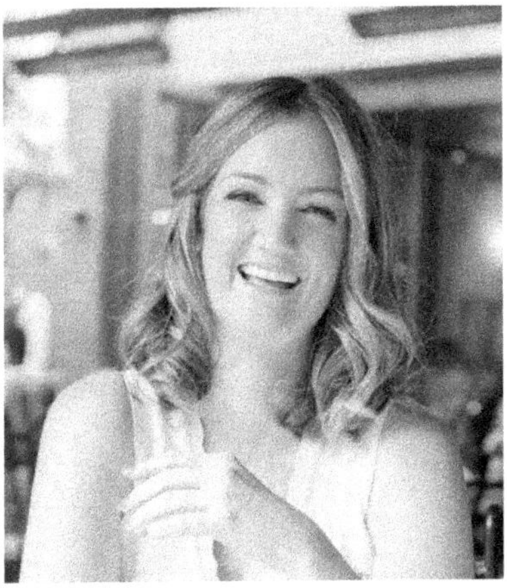

Jaimie Sarah is the Founder of Definitely Definitely and the Creator of The Aligned Business Blueprint®, Business The Aligned Way® and The 6 Types of Content To Captivate and Convert™. She helps extraordinary service-based experts and companies to attract, convert and retain more high calibre clients with integrity.

She does this by helping them become more aligned in their marketing messaging, their offerings and their ways of being (their energy) for optimal results. She also offers highly exclusive agency services for 7 and 8-figure+ businesses seeking on-brand, "done for you" marketing content.

Jaimie is the host of The Jaimie Sarah Show Podcast and has been featured in Forbes, Thrive Global, The Express and more, and named Executive Coach of The Year in the UK for 3 years running.

Find her at www.jaimiesarah.com

facebook.com/definitelydefinitely
instagram.com/definitely_definitely
linkedin.com/in/jaimiesarah

CPSIA information can be obtained
at www.ICGtesting.com
Printed in the USA
LVHW080745221222
735594LV00035B/522/J

9 781915 771070